TWAYNE'S WORLD AUTHORS SERIES

A Survey of the World's Literature

Sylvia E. Bowman, Indiana University

GENERAL EDITOR

DENMARK and NORWAY

Leif Sjöberg, SUNY at Stony Brook

EDITOR

Ludvig Holberg

TWAS 321

Engraving 1731 by Christian Fritzsch
Photograph courtesy of the Royal Danish
Ministry for Foreign Affairs

Ludvig Holberg

Ludvig Holberg

By F. J. BILLESKOV JANSEN

University of Copenhagen

Twayne Publishers, Inc.   ::   New York

Library of Congress Cataloging in Publication Data

Jansen, Frederik Julius Billeskov, 1907–
  Ludvig Holberg.

  (Twayne's world authors series, TWAS 321)
  Bibliography: p. 129.
  1. Holberg, Ludvig, Baron, 1684–1754.
PT8087.J3   839.8'1'8409   74-2171
ISBN 0-8057-2431-1

Contents

About the Author

Preface

Chronology

1. The Age of Holberg   13

2. Years of Youth   22

3. Travels in the Latin World   36

4. A Poet Is Born   44

5. Comedies   56

6. The Autobiography of a Man in His Prime   82

7. From Dramatist to Historian   89

8. The Struggle for Tolerance   98

9. The Revival of the Theater   108

10. Sorø Academy   123

Selected Bibliography   129

Index   133

About the Author

F. J. Billeskov Jansen is Professor of Danish Literature at the University of Copenhagen. He received his doctorate at the same university with a thesis on Ludvig Holberg and later edited a series of annotated editions of Holberg's works. In his writings he has emphasized the European background of Holberg's contribution to literature.

Dr. Billeskov Jansen participated for a number of years in the work of the Executive Committee of the International Comparative Literature Association and of the International Association for Germanic Studies. In the first year of issue (1973) of *Neohelicon* (The Hague-Paris-Budapest) he gave a survey of *Studies in Comparative Literature within Scandinavian Countries*. Dr. Billeskov Jansen has particular links with French cultural life. His first book, *Sources vives de la pensée de Montaigne* (1935), was on the life and work of Montaigne, and he has published in French a theory of the nature and function of literature: *Esthétique de l'Œuvre d'art littéraire* (1948). He was co-founder of *Orbis Litterarum International Review of Literary Studies* and is co-editor and co-author of *Verdenslitteraturhistorie*, a history of world literature appearing in 12 volumes in Danish 1971–1974.

Preface

Within the last dozen years or so, three of Ludvig Holberg's major works have been published in English translation. In 1960 Holberg's imaginary journey, *Niels Klim*, appeared. This was both his work of social criticism and his Utopia. In 1962 came his long mock-heroic poem, *Peder Paars*, a treasury of comical situations, and in 1970 a fine edition of Holberg's fascinating and enjoyable *Memoirs*. Ludvig Holberg is thus very much present in the Anglo-Saxon world, and this is an encouragement to anyone attempting to provide an introduction to his life and letters. In this presentation of him, specimens running to several pages are given of Holberg's prose and verse, but it is good to know that interested readers can proceed to the translations now available, if they wish to read more. As appears from the bibliography at the end of the book, only about half of Holberg's comedies have been translated into English (many are still in print). It is much to be desired, however, that a complete translation of the comedies be made. It is a pity, too, that Holberg's main philosophical work, *Moral Thoughts*, has never been translated into English.

Thus, my little monograph is not entering a vacuum: particularly in the United States there seems to be a growing interest in the man who founded modern Danish and Norwegian literature. From the present book it can be seen that he was right at the center of his age, vitally concerned with contributing to enlightenment and progress. In Scandinavia Holberg's age is the Age of the Enlightenment. But Ludvig Holberg also has a place in the long history of Denmark and Norway.

Once again it is very fortunate that recently Professor P. M. Mitchell, of the University of Illinois, and I were able to publish *Anthology of Danish Literature* (Southern Illinois University Press, 1971), a work of 600 pages containing significant Danish texts from the Middle Ages to recent times. The foreword to that volume contains these words: "He who reads in this book can scarcely avoid feeling that a thousand-year-old kingdom lives in these pages. This anthology takes into account not only literary and aesthetic material; it would also give insight into the cultural life in the course of several centuries." The anthology is bilingual, so that it may serve not only as an introduction to the reading of Danish literature, but also to the study of the Danish language in all its phases.

On concluding my labors with this book, I wish to thank Professor Leif Sjöberg, of the State University of New York at Stony Brook, who conveyed to me the request to write a monograph on Holberg for Twayne's World Authors Series. I also wish to thank Mrs. Karen Prytz' Legat for support during the work, and also the University of Nebraska Press and The American-Scandinavian Foundation for permission to quote from the translation of *Peder Paars*. Last but not least, I thank David Stoner, M.A., who has not only translated my text but has also rendered into his mother tongue some of the excerpts from Holberg's writings that appear in this book.

F. J. BILLESKOV JANSEN

Copenhagen, Denmark

Chronology

1684	Ludvig Holberg was born in Bergen, Norway, on December 3.
1686	L. H.'s father, Lieutenant-Colonel Christian Nielsen Holberg, died, about 65 years old, on March 29.
1694	L. H. entered Bergen Cathedral School.
1695	L. H.'s mother died in an epidemic.
1695–1698 (?)	L. H. stayed with his mother's cousin, Otto Munthe, who was parish priest in Fron, in Gudbrandsdalen, Norway.
1698 (?)–1702	L. H. stayed with his maternal uncle, Peder Lem, a merchant in Bergen.
1702	The fire of Bergen, May 19.
1702	L. H. matriculated at the University of Copenhagen in July.
1702	L. H. returned to Bergen in the fall and soon after became tutor in the house of Dean Weinwich at Voss.
1703	L. H. came to Copenhagen in the fall.
1704	L. H. passed the philosophical examination (metaphysics, ethics, etc.) at the University, March 10.
1704	L. H. passed the theological examination, April.
1704	In the fall L. H. was tutor in the house of Niels Smed, the Deputy Bishop of Bergen.
1704–1705	L. H. spent about a year traveling in Holland.
1705	L. H. arrived at Kristianssand ca. October 1.
1706	Visit to England (London, Oxford) in April.
1708	L. H. returned to Copenhagen during the summer.
1708	L. H. in October traveled to Dresden and Leipzig as mentor for the son of Professor Poul Winding.
1709	L. H. in January (?) returned to Copenhagen and became tutor to the sons of Admiral Giedde.
1709–1714	L. H. was a scholar at Borchs Kollegium.
1711	Publication of L. H.'s first book, *Introduction to the History of the Principal Kingdoms of Europe.*
1714	L. H. was promised a professorship.
1714	L. H. in the spring traveled via Holland to Paris.

1715	L. H. in August sailed by river to Marseilles, then on to Rome via Genoa.
1716	L. H. in February walked through Italy, across the Alps, and through France to Paris.
1716	L. H. traveled via Amsterdam and Hamburg to Copenhagen in the spring.
1716	Publication of *Introduction to Natural Law and the Law of Nations*.
1717	L. H. was appointed as Professor of Metaphysics and Logic in December.
1719	L. H. published two fictitious polemical disputations against the historian and jurist Andreas Hojer.
1719–1720	Publication of *Peder Paars*.
1720	L. H. in May was appointed Professor of Latin Literature.
1722	The theater opened in the street of Lille Grønnegade, September 23.
1723–1725	Comedies I–V.
1725	L. H. traveled via Hamburg and Amsterdam to Paris in the summer.
1726	L. H. in February traveled home from Paris via Amsterdam and Hamburg.
1728	The theater in Lille Grønnegade closed, on February 25. However, a few performances took place in the summer of 1728, and on October 11 the troupe acted before the court at Copenhagen Castle.
1728	Publication of the first part of L. H.'s *Memoirs*.
1728	Publication of *Conversations* on the subject of the Danish East India Company and Copenhagen import monopolies.
1728	The fire of Copenhagen, October 20–22.
1729	Publication of *Description of Denmark and Norway*.
1730	L. H. was appointed Professor of History.
1731	Publication of *The Danish Stage* I–V.
1732–1735	Publication of *History of the Kingdom of Denmark*.
1735–1736	L. H. was rector of Copenhagen University and on May 31, 1736, gave his valedictory address.
1737	Publication of *Short Latin Works*, which included the first two parts of L. H.'s *Memoirs* and his Latin epigrams.
1737	L. H. became quaestor, i.e. bursar, of the University and was exempted from lecturing duties.
1737	Publication of *Description of Bergen*, in April.

Chronology

1738	Publication of *General Church History*, in June.
1739	Publication of *Comparative Histories of Heroes*, in March.
1740	L. H. purchased the estate of Brorup near Slagelse.
1741	Publication of *Niels Klim*, in the spring.
1742	Publication of *Jewish History*, in March.
1743	Publication of a new volume of *Short Latin Works* containing the third part of *Memoirs* and fresh Latin epigrams.
1744	Publication of *Moral Thoughts*, in January.
1745	Publication of *Comparative Histories of Heroines*, in February.
1745	L. H. purchased the estate of Tersløsegaard near Sorø.
1746	Publication of *Reflections on the Cattle Disease now Prevailing*.
1746	Publication, in December, of L. H.'s translation of Herodian with an introduction *On the Cause of the Immense Expansion of Rome*.
1748–1750	Publication of *Epistles* I–IV.
1751	Publication of *Moral Fables*, in January.
1751	L. H., in April, resigned from office as quaestor of the University.
1753–1754	Publication of *The Danish Stage* VI–VII.
1754	L. H. died in Copenhagen, on January 28.
1754	Publication of *Epistles* V, in September.
1754	L. H.'s coffin, in December, was placed in the convent church of Sorø.

CHAPTER 1

The Age of Holberg

TO Danes and Norwegians the first half of the eighteenth century is the Age of Ludvig Holberg. Holberg was molded by the age in which he lived, but he in his turn also left his mark upon it: he was both the child and the father of his age. If the reader is unacquainted with Scandinavian history, it will be important to place the age in its historical setting and provide him with some of that background knowledge which, as Hans Christian Andersen says in *Sorrow of Heart*, is so useful.

I *The Dual Monarchy and Absolutism*

For the benefit of such readers we can say that the dual monarchy, of which Ludvig Holberg was the greatest son, was a political reality from 1380 to 1814. Until they were gathered into three countries—Denmark and Norway in the ninth century and Sweden in the eleventh century—the Scandinavian lands consisted of petty kingdoms. For well over a century, 1389–1523, all three countries were united under the Danish crown. Concurrent with Sweden's secession from the Nordic union was the arrival of Lutheranism in Scandinavia, and at the same time, too, the royal power increased, not least under Christian IV, who was King of Denmark-Norway from 1588 to 1648. Sweden grew into a great power under King Gustavus II Adolphus, who fell in battle against Wallenstein at Lützen in 1632. The rivalry between Denmark-Norway and Sweden led to some bloody clashes. The Dano-Norwegian state was in a position to seal off Sweden's access to the Kattegat and the North Sea. But in 1658 a Swedish army compelled Denmark to cede the provinces to the east of the Øresund, and from that time these provinces (Skåne, Halland, Blekinge) were part of southern

13

Sweden. In this way Danish control of Swedish ports was broken. The following year the Swedish king tried to conquer Copenhagen, but was repulsed.

During these dramatic events the Dano-Norwegian king, Frederik III, and the burghers of Copenhagen had become allies, and by a joint *coup d'état* they introduced absolute monarchy into Denmark and Norway in 1660–61. The old nobility was prepared to accept having its influence curtailed to a minimum. The first absolute hereditary kings, Christian V (1670–99) and Frederik IV (1699–1730) surrounded themselves with a pomp and glitter modeled on the Versailles of Louis XIV. They made vigorous but unsuccessful attempts to reconquer the lost eastern provinces, first in the Skåne War 1675–79 and then in the Great Northern War 1700–1720. After the latter, which brings us right up to Holberg's time, all hope of reconquest was abandoned.

Thus, 1720 is in many ways a watershed date in the history of Denmark. The wars had drained the resources of Denmark and Norway. But since there was peace from that time right down to the Napoleonic Wars, trade and industry began to thrive, and, as a consequence of absolutism, the lion's share of the increased wealth of the country fell to the middle classes. These were times of prosperity for the clergy and government officials, for merchants and master craftsmen. There were also other prizes to strive for. Absolutism established a rigid order of social rank, and it became the ambition of the free burghers to rise in rank and be received into the new nobility that the king was establishing in competition with the old. This was the political, social, and economic pattern which Holberg entered and in which he made his way. He obtained a well-paid post as a professor; he was shrewd enough to make money from his books; and he ended up as a baron and a benefactor of the state. Absolutism had provided new openings for poetic, scholarly, and practical gifts such as his.

Holberg had good reason to be satisfied with the status quo. He did not, like Voltaire, Montesquieu, and Rousseau, pave the way for any revolution. For him the remodeling of the state system that had taken place in 1660 was a beneficial revolution, a useful and necessary fact of life. But of course, as we shall see, this did not restrain him from ridiculing the state, the church, and the judicial system of his native land in a comic epic, nor from mocking the rank-hungry bourgeoisie in a comedy.

II A Rococo Capital: Copenhagen

To a great degree the dispositions of the successive absolute monarchs set the tone for the whole country. Frederik IV possessed an easy and outgoing temperament, and entertainments, particularly the theater, benefited from this. His son, Christian VI (1730–46) was a gloomy introvert with religious anxieties and gauche manners. The nation was under restraint until his son, Frederik V (1746–66), who took after his grandfather, brought gaiety to court and country once more.

But common to all the kings of Holberg's age was a delight in building castles, and as this was an outstanding period for European architecture, and gifted Scandinavian architects were given the means to make extensive travels, some of the results were exceedingly beautiful. Even today the castles that have been preserved from that time still give Copenhagen and its environs a late baroque and rococo aura. In 1700–1709 Frederiksberg Castle was erected as a summer residence in a late and harmonious baroque style. When peace was concluded in 1720, Frederik IV could afford to build, in the countryside of Zealand, the castle of Fredensborg, extensively laid out in Italian baroque style. In 1732–34 his successor, Christian VI, had the graceful hunting lodge Eremitage erected, and this still stands in the middle of one of greater Copenhagen's open spaces looking out over grassland on which deer graze.

Unfortunately, the two most grandiose building projects of Christian VI no longer exist. One of these was Hirschholm Castle, a fairy-tale castle in North Zealand, which proved to have unstable foundations and was pulled down in 1810–12. The other was the royal residence of Christiansborg, which was erected in the center of the capital, in a flamboyant rococo style; this burned down in 1794, but its monumental wings around the riding-ground and the connecting marble bridge still stand. Opposite to it lies Prinsens Palæ, erected in 1743–44

for the future Frederik V. When he came to the throne he went
further than any of the others by assigning to the royal architect,
Nicolai Eigtved, the task of creating a completely new quarter
of the city, which was to bear the name of Frederiksstaden.
Today it is one of Europe's outstanding rococo creations. Its
center was an octagonal piazza with four identical mansions
around it. The land was made available without cost to four
noble families, who in 1749–60 paid for the erection of the
mansions. After Christiansborg burned down in 1794, the royal
family began to move into Amalienborg, which became the
name for the entire complex of four mansions and is still the
royal residence. From the piazza radiated streets that were
lined mainly with the town houses of the rich built in related
architectural styles. A projected church, the Marble Church, was
not, however, completed until 1894. But in 1771, after many
years of preparation, one of the most distinguished equestrian
statues in the world was unveiled, created by the Frenchman
Saly and depicting the founder of Frederiksstaden, King Frederik V. However, this statue, which is, as it were, the copestone
of the monumental Copenhagen of Holberg's age, came too
late for Holberg to see, as he died in 1754. But when we stand
at the foot of this statue, we can rejoice at the sense of
beautiful proportions, of symmetry, and of order that charac-
terizes Danish baroque. The piazza at the center of Amalienborg Palace is rightly regarded as one of the most beautiful
in the world.

Ornate gardens were another rococo manifestation in Denmark.
The people of Holberg's age did not seek nature wild and
untrammeled; they created their own tasteful, but strictly
tamed, natural beauty. One of the lyric poets of the age,
Ambrosius Stub (1705–58), an itinerant poet, gracefully sketched
the small-scale nature to be seen during a walk outside the
city one spring day. "Den kedsom Vinter gik sin Gang" (The
Irksome Winter Went His Way) tells us that spring has come,
so we should arise and go out to see how beautifully laughing
nature is behaving. The features of nature reborn are completely
human: the dawn sun rising with long beams in his hair; as
the shepherd boy blows his horn, the forest echo makes answer;
spring has decked out the beech tree as a bride; and in the

noontide heat the sun spreads fire through bosom and vitals. Evening draws on, the lake still stands like a mirror, so that the sun can see his own image in it. I must think of my bed and return home with thoughts of the Creator, whose providence can be traced in the sky, on earth, and in the water.

III *The Age of Enlightenment and Pietism*

In the eighteenth century the Germanic and Nordic world shared in the movement known as the Enlightenment, which had been initiated particularly by France and England. In his *Discours de la méthode* (1637) the philosopher and mathematician René Descartes expressed a confidence in the ability of reason to differentiate between false and true, and this confidence was confirmed by Isaac Newton's brilliant advances in the realm of physics and mathematics. Rational criticism regarded no area as sacred; it assailed the orthodoxy of the Church and, with Pierre Bayle, who was born in France but had to live in the Netherlands, demonstrated how anti-rational and inhumane was the Catholic Church's persecution of divergent views. A criticism of the biblical texts was established, and there arose a tendency to explain away miracles and anti-rational dogmas. All over Europe there gradually came to be many adherents of a pared-down Christianity—deism—reduced to a belief in God as Creator, who would punish and reward all men after death according to their deserts.

But it must be stressed that in Germany and the North, the belief in reason, rationalism, encountered, struggled with, and mingled with a powerful emotional movement, pietism. Rationalism was the rebellion of the intellect against dogmatism of all kinds. Pietism was the protest of the heart against a Christianity that had congealed into orthodoxy. The German pietists demanded that each Christian should undergo a personal crisis marking his passing from perfunctory Christian observance to full devotion to Christ. While rationalistic Christianity shed layer after layer of dogma, pietists reveled in the mystery of salvation through the sacrificial death of Christ. It may be said that for rationalism the twin ideas of sin and grace had ceased to exist, whereas for the pietists this antithesis meant everything.

There was, however, one thing that pietism and Enlightenment had in common: their interest in schools and education. Even though their aims were different, both movements regarded knowledge as necessary for the individual's religious development. The pietists wanted to quicken and vitalize Christian doctrine; education should aim at forming the kingdom of God in the hearts of the young. The men of the Enlightenment wanted to prevent men, through ignorance, from falling victims to anti-rational superstition sweeping them along into intolerant actions. In Holberg, as we shall see, the points of contrast between these movements are much more obvious than the points of agreement.

In Danish literature pietism assumed an outstanding position by virtue of the gifted hymn writer, Hans Adolph Brorson (1694–1764). He was born in southern Jutland, in the area by way of which German pietism infiltrated successfully into Denmark. He came of a clerical family, and he himself became a clergyman in Tønder, where services were held in both German and Danish. At that time the leading churchman in Tønder, the dean, was the German-speaking Johann Herman Schrader. In 1729, when Brorson came to Tønder, Schrader was just completing a large hymnbook pervaded by a pietistic spirit, and this was published in 1731. Inspired by this, Brorson wrote for his Danish congregation some small collections of hymns, of which the first appeared at Christmas, 1732. So many followed, that in 1739 Brorson was able to gather them, along with several additional original hymns and translations, under the title *Troens rare Klenodie* (The Rare Jewel of Faith). In this are hymns that have become the cherished possessions of Danish congregations. Among them is:

> Den yndigste Rose er funden
> blandt stiveste Torne oprunden,
> Vor Jesus den dejligste Pode
> Blandt syndige Mennesker groede.

> (There blossoms the best of all roses
> Where proudest of thornkind encloses;
> Our Jesus, a rosebud so winning,
> Was circled by men who were sinning.)

The picture given by this hymn is that the world of men is a garden of roses, which, since the Fall, has grown rank and wild. In this sin-ravaged wilderness a noble rose grows up; Jesus is conceived as the rose from whom shoots are grafted onto the misshapen bushes, so that they regain their original noble nature. These are the saved, but many harden themselves against the rose that brings salvation. They are "thistle minds" stiff-necked and proud like thorns. In the stanza that is to call these unbending souls to repentance, the poet-clergyman with fervent imagery shows that "the lowly position" represents both the humble, kneeling posture of the penitent sinner, and the valleys where the roses grow:

> Ach søger de nedrige Steder,
> I Støvet for Frelseren græder,
> Saa faa I vor Jesum i Tale,
> Thi Roserne vokser i Dale.

> (Ah, seek out the lowly position;
> Abased, show the Saviour contrition,
> Sweet converse with Jesus will follow,
> For roses grow down in the hollow.)

It was this verse that Hans Christian Andersen used, rather freely, as a recurrent theme in his tale "The Snow Queen."

Many of Brorson's pietistic hymns deal with the struggle and victory of faith. In one hymn the convert triumphs: "Halleluja, I have found my Jesus." And in this same hymn Søren Kierkegaard found the verse that he selected for his tombstone:

> Det er en liden Tid
> Saa har jeg vunden,
> Saa er den ganske Strid
> Med ét forsvunden,
> Saa kan jeg hvile mig
> I Rosen-Sale
> Og uafledelig
> Min Jesum tale.

> (The time is yet but short
> Ere warfare's vanished,

> My battles — now fierce-fought —
> By vict'ry banished.
> In roseate halls at peace
> I'll rest unseeking,
> There I shall never cease
> With Jesus speaking.)

In 1737 Brorson moved to Ribe to be dean, and in 1741 he became bishop in the same city. In his closing years he rediscovered poetry, not now as hymns for the church, but as songs for private devotions. Illness, personal sorrows, and anxiety about the advance of worldliness weighed upon his mind. Brorson was very musical and himself played upon the lute. He now wrote pious refrains and arias that appeared after his death in 1765 under the title *Svane-Sang* (Swan Song). Everywhere in Brorson's poetry we can admire the ease and naturalness with which he shaped his verses. But in *Swan Song* the naturalness becomes virtuosity. Brorson has a predilection for complicated verse forms and clothes these forms with dazzling ease. As often with the pietists, a basic theme is borrowed from the dialogue of the Canticles between bridegroom and bride, taken to symbolize Jesus and the individual soul. In the finest and most fervent of them, we are left to supply the speakers ourselves. This song will be quoted in the translation of R. P. Keigwin (from his anthology *In Denmark I Was Born*). We shall see that, like Ambrosius Stub's poem, this song is a springtime wandering, but here just at the transition from winter to the first tender and fragile spring.

We are still in winter. The bridegroom, Jesus, exhorts his bride, the soul, to have patience:

> Now no murmur, bide but firmer,
> bide but firmer, O faint of soul.

And yet, the bride laments aloud:

> Times that chasten seldom hasten,
> seldom hasten, 'tis not their way.
> As the days lengthen, winter will strengthen,
> winter will strengthen and bring dismay.

> Times that chasten seldom hasten,
> seldom hasten, 'tis not their way.

But then the bridegroom informs his turtledove that she can see the first green shoots, harbingers of early summer. In delight the bride exclaims:

> Ah, that blossom sweet on bosom,
> sweet on bosom of gentle spring!
> Now we may shiver, shudder and quiver —
> shudder and quiver, they soon take wing.

The bridegroom is still full of hope, although the cold comes and the snow still covers the early flowers, and finally he can triumphantly call upon his beloved to show herself as the dove in Noah's Ark with an olive leaf in her beak. For now the glad hour of liberation is at hand.

Once, when the Danish nation was feeling the cold of winter in its heart, a line from this poem by Brorson had a profound effect. It was during the second year of the German occupation. It was September 26, 1941, King Christian X's birthday. A large gathering of people were standing in front of the palace of Amalienborg to pay homage. From the balcony of the palace the king made a brief speech, which he opened by quoting the lines "times that chasten seldom hasten":

> Trange Tider langsomt skrider —

This book will be entirely devoted to presenting Holberg, but it is important for the reader to recall Brorson at the same time. It will add an extra dimension to the reading if it is borne in mind that Holberg's half century was also that of Brorson.

CHAPTER 2

Years of Youth

LUDVIG Holberg was born in Bergen, Norway, on December 3, 1684. His father, Christian Nielsen Holberg, born about 1620, probably came of peasant stock. He had served in the army and had worked his way up from a private to the rank of lieutenant colonel. According to all evidence he was a brave and honorable man, and Ludvig Holberg was justly proud of his father. Together with Cort Adeler, a Danish naval warrior, he served with the Venetians against the Turks, and when the war was over he walked his way right through Italy purely for his own pleasure. In 1656 he even enrolled at the University of Siena. He married late (in 1667), and at his death in 1686 he left six children, of whom the youngest, Ludvig, was scarcely eighteen months old. Holberg's mother, Karen Lem, came of a clerical family, being the daughter of Peder Lem, a prosperous parish priest at Fana outside Bergen. This family included several men of education, but none of them wrote anything of consequence. Holberg does not seem to have inherited his urge to write; he was the first literary figure in the family. Two of Holberg's great-grandparents may perhaps be mentioned: Karen Lem's grandfather, Niels Pedersen Lem, who died about 1636, a considerable landowner, was a man of some education. He compiled a dictionary of Dano-Norwegian legal terms, which was never printed, but which found a place in the comprehensive collection of Icelandic and Norwegian manuscripts founded by Árni Magnússon in Copenhagen. The manuscript of the dictionary is still to be found there. Holberg could thus easily have got hold of his great-grandfather's work, and it might well have amused him to compare it with Christen Osterson Weile's Danish legal glossary, printed in 1641, which he subjects to rather harsh criticism in his Epistle 527. Karen Lem's maternal grandfather, Ludvig Munthe, had been Bishop of Bergen, and Holberg was named for him. He published only one independent work, and if Holberg read it, he was probably not particularly proud of the pious superstition expressed in this short composition entitled *A True Account of Some Strange and Remarkable Births in the Diocese of Bergen with Some Simple Instruction as to What We Should Call to Mind on the Occasion of Such Monstrous Births* (1641). Ludvig Stoud, a cousin of Holberg's mother, may also be mentioned; he became Bishop of Kristianssand and composed a few printed and unprinted sermons.

Ludvig Holberg's mother died in 1695 and the children were scattered "like wild birds," as Holberg's sister Sophie later expressed it in a petition to the king. Ludvig, who had first attended the German school for boys in Bergen and later the grammar school (Latinskolen), spent some time in the Valley of Gudsbrandsdalen with a cousin of his mother's, but probably in 1698 returned to Bergen, and here Peder Lem, his uncle and guardian, who was a merchant, took care of him. This enterprising and merry uncle was exactly after his nephew's heart. Once, as a rash young student of Latin, Ludvig had written a satirical poem about one of the ladies of the family. She complained to the head of the household, demanding punishment. The uncle took the cheeky youngster into another room and began to upbraid him harshly, but it soon transpired that these remonstrances were not directed at the content of the poem but at its form. The only exhortation given to the young man was to pay more attention to the rules of meter in future!

Holberg, then, grew up in Bergen in the midst of the capable and affluent burghers of that city. He was himself to show outstanding business acumen. The rector of the grammar school, Søren Lintrup, was a man of considerable initiative. He was later to become a professor and a bishop. On May 19, 1702, a fire broke out and reduced most of Bergen to ashes, including Peder Lem's house and the grammar school. The rector made a rapid decision to conclude the teaching of the senior class, and so by July 20 of that same year Holberg had matriculated at the University of Copenhagen. Thus a disaster had put a hasty end to his first youth. From then on he was left to his own resources, and it was rather a long time before he found his niche. He stayed in Copenhagen only a few months. Short of money, he returned to Bergen and from there moved on to Voss, to the northeast of Bergen, as tutor and spiritual assistant in the house of Weinwich, the rural dean there. Since 1697 students had been permitted to preach in village churches. This was the only period of his life in which Holberg preached from the pulpit and, according to Epistle 85, he spoke very briefly— once for only fifteen minutes. It is uncertain when Holberg returned to Copenhagen. In March-April, 1704, he took the degree examination in theology and philosophy. Thus, at the age of 19½, he had his theological qualifications and could prepare for a career as a grammar-school teacher or in the church. But his stay at Voss seems to have given him a distaste for both teaching and preaching.

I *To the Netherlands and to England*

Since his eighteenth birthday Holberg had been master of a small inheritance from his parents. If he had felt a desire to become a scholar, he could probably have used these resources to study further in Copenhagen or abroad. But Holberg now returned to Bergen, where he became a tutor in the house of the suffragan bishop, Niels Smed. In his youth this man had traveled extensively in Germany, Italy, France, and the Netherlands. Holberg was given leave to read his travel diary and was seized by an irresistible urge to get out and about himself. In spite of his family's opposition he sold the land he had inherited and traveled to the Netherlands with sixty rix-dollars in his purse. This money was quickly spent. During the journey he was possibly in the service of a Russian nobleman for a time, perhaps as a language teacher.

From Holberg's frank *Memoirs* we can see that he did not travel to the Netherlands with the intention of studying, and indeed he took learning fairly lightly in these youthful years. Later he relates that one of his teachers at school gave all his pupils the advice to read the newspapers assiduously. Holberg adds: "I paid great attention to this exhortation and was therefore much acclaimed amongst the common people as a great politician." (*Moral Thoughts.* 1943 ed., p. 281). When writing about his journey to the Netherlands in his *Memoirs,* Holberg describes himself as having a mind thirsting for all kind of new things: "animus novitatis avidus." This was the young Holberg, then, always eager for the news of the day and now itching to travel. In Holland he suffered some privation and hunger, and when he made a detour into Germany to Aachen, he tried to slip away from his hotel early in the morning without paying, but he was caught by the landlord and had to pay every penny. On borrowed money he returned rather sheepishly to Norway.

Had Holberg derived any profit from his rash trip to the Netherlands? Yes, he had seen a city of international standing. To a man from Bergen, Copenhagen with its 70,000 inhabitants probably seemed a city of some size, but the population of Amsterdam was 200,000, and in this city Holberg feasted his eyes, as he himself tells us, on all that the Netherlands had to boast of. In Holberg's youth the Netherlands was still looked up to as a great power. Its navy had been admired in Denmark and Norway since the time of King Christian IV (1588–1648), and it had not been forgotten that under King Frederik III (1648–70) it had saved Copenhagen when it was threatened by the Swedes in 1658. Merchants from the Netherlands had close connections with Scandinavia. Dutch architecture exerted a great influence upon Danish architecture. Dutch literature was translated into Danish; the Dutch language was understood not only on the quayside in Bergen but also in Danish ports. In *The Fortunate Shipwreck,* a comedy Holberg was later to write, one character, Henrik, pretends to be a Dutch sailor, and both master and servants understand his speech without difficulty. The Netherlands and the Dutch language had a position in Denmark-Norway at that time approximating to that of England and English in present-day Denmark. So it is scarcely remarkable that Holberg's first journey abroad was to the Netherlands.

His ignominious return from his travels did not encourage him to go back to Bergen, so instead he went to Kristianssand, where he spent the winter of 1705–1706 with Otto Stoud, a curate who was Holberg's cousin and the son of Bishop Stoud

mentioned above, who had recently died. Otto Stoud's unmarried sister Sophie, who was two years Holberg's junior,
was living in the house. Holberg describes her as unusually
beautiful, and he is altogether much occupied with young
ladies in his account of the pleasant time he spent at Kristianssand. It would seem quite probable that he was rather attracted
to his beautiful second cousin, but nevertheless in the spring of
1706, when another chance of foreign travel came his way, he
did not hesitate to take it. In Kristianssand, Kristian Brix, a
graduate in theology of Holberg's own age, talked him into
a plan for traveling to England, and so he came to spend the
next two and a half years there.

It is plain that this time Holberg was traveling with a quite
different purpose in mind. After the voyage across the North Sea
the two friends immediately went on from London to Oxford,
so it is clear that Holberg had not come to England to see
another great city, but to study. At that time Oxford was the
place to go to read books. For among the few libraries in Europe
with public access, the Bodleian Library was one of the most
famous. We find, for instance, that during the period 1683–1708
no fewer than sixty-two Danes, Norwegians, and Holsteiners
entered their names in the register of the Bodleian Library.
Among these was, for example, Frederik Rostgaard (whose
name will recur later), who stayed in Oxford for ten months in
1693–94. Then, too, in the Royal Library in Copenhagen there
is a manuscript travel diary in which the author, who was
obviously given permission to examine the register, notes that
"from nowhere are there more names than from Denmark."
He recounts that on July 17, 1714, he swore an oath that he
would not steal or damage the books and thereupon kissed the
Bible placed before him. (From the register we can deduce
that this traveling scholar, whose name does not occur in the
manuscript, was a young theologian, J. J. Sevel, born in 1694,
who on his return was designated professor, but died in 1728 as
chaplain at Frederiksborg Castle). This manuscript supplements
Holberg's own account of his travels. He and Brix swore their
oaths on April 18, 1706, and signed their names, paying a fee
which left a large hole in their funds. They tried to make
ends meet by giving lessons in music and languages, as Hol-

berg recounts in his *Memoirs*: "He described himself as a musi-
cian and I described myself as a grammarian, but the misfortune
was that he was as little a master in his profession as I in mine."
They were therefore soon obliged to make their way on foot
to London so that Brix could raise a loan, for which a Norwegian
stood surety. For a month they lived well in London, and then
returned to Oxford. Holberg relates: "When we had returned we
could not support such a lonely life any longer, but moved into
an inn frequented by many Oxford undergraduates, and before
long we were acquainted with them all and familiar friends of
some. Only a Scot, who had previously been a close friend of
ours, began to treat us coldly from that time. For long the cause
of this was unknown to us, but when we asked him the reason
for his altered attitude, he warned us sincerely that we should
seek another lodging, as it was unbecoming for students to lodge
at an inn—it was at least unusual at Oxford." Before long, however, Brix was ordered back to London. His wealthy mother in
Trondheim had probably heard about the secured loan and
placed her son under the surveillance of Georg Ursin, the Danish
pastor in London.

So once more Holberg had to manage quite alone, but
unlike his situation in Amsterdam where he had been one insig-
nificant academic among ships' captains and other men of authority, in England he was among equals who knew how to pay
generously for instruction in languages and music and were too
polite to say so openly even when his teaching was deficient.
Indeed Holberg came to know many sides of the English character. He became acquainted with its generosity and delicacy of
feeling; thus almost every day he was asked to dinner at a
college, and when his departure was imminent the undergraduates of Magdalen College in tactful terms offered him money
for the journey, but he did not need to accept. It is plain from
the *Memoirs* that Holberg really had a taste for the comradely
good fellowship of the colleges and the inns as well as of the
Musical Club, of which, to his gratification, he was made a
member and where he played every Wednesday. Commenting
on university life in Oxford, he writes: "There can be almost
no university at which the students show such respect for
authority and for the rules and where they live such honorable,

well-conducted, and Christian lives as at Oxford. There, even
the slightest error is severely regarded, corrected, and punished.
It is therefore as beneficial for the young to be sent to Oxford
as it is harmful for them to be sent to other universities, at
which, as well as their studies, they learn to gamble and drink!"
He found the English rather boastful of their virtues and generally prone to arrogance, but admired their candor and good
spirits. He also noticed a different emphasis on some aspects
of university life upon which great stress was laid at Copenhagen. The general standard of Latin at Oxford, particularly
spoken Latin, was low, and little attention was paid to the art
of disputing. He noted too that the English were less concerned
with gaining a wide and superficial knowledge, but slowly and
thoroughly penetrated more deeply into matters that concerned
them. In these few shrewd comments we can see that Holberg's
critical observation, later to find expression in his moral writings,
was making the most of this opportunity to regard another
nation's ways and thoughts and, by comparison, to evaluate the
standards to which he was accustomed.

In *Moral Thoughts* Holberg was later to write: "In my youth
I was an avid newspaper reader, but later I abandoned this object
of study, and went over to another kind of reading matter which
I considered of more solid value." It can be presumed that it was
while he was staying in Kristianssand that he realized that newspapers were not enough, and that solid reading of serious books
was required. And then he came to Oxford, where the books
were available to him, and here he realized that his way ahead
lay through authorship. In the Bodleian he became aware of his
vocation: he was seized by the urge to write. Among those many
books, he says in his *Memoirs*, "I was struck by the ambitious
thought of becoming an author at an early age." And so he
decided to write an instructive work, a geography of each of
the countries of Europe followed by an outline of its history.
And so he spent his time in Oxford preparing this work.

Before returning to Scandinavia Holberg once more spent a
short time in London, where his only experience of interest seems
to have been a visit to a Baptists' meetinghouse, where he wit-
nessed the baptism of an old woman. He would seem to have
gained no lasting impression of the new critical and philosophical

trends in English thought which were later to be of such profound significance for Holberg himself and for the whole cultural development of Denmark-Norway.

II A Start as an Author

Holberg, then, returned to Copenhagen, and was once more penniless. He tried to gain an income by lecturing to students on conditions abroad. They listened eagerly enough, but they did not pay. In 1708 Holberg was given the task of accompanying the son of Poul Winding, a wealthy professor, to Dresden. With his earnings from this he traveled on to Leipzig, where he entered into the gay student life there and visited professors who received strangers hospitably. When he returned home he was once more obliged to be a tutor for a time, but then Professor Winding obtained for him a lodging in a college, Borchs Kollegium, where he remained from 1709 to 1714. It was now time for him to reap the harvest of his labors at Oxford. But on his return from England he had discovered to his annoyance that during his absence a rather similar book had appeared by H. O. Pflug entitled *The Danish Pilgrim, or a General Geography and Brief Historical Description of the Whole Known World.* Holberg therefore decided to make two books of his one manuscript, so in 1711 there appeared the "improved" (which probably means expanded) historical section and in 1713, as an appendix to this, some of the geographical material. But whereas the former sold, though slowly, the latter seems to have had little success, and the greater part of the manuscript lay unprinted and has therefore been lost.

He took as his model for the whole book *An Introduction to the History of the Principal Kingdoms* by the German Samuel Pufendorf, written in 1682. Holberg entitled his book *Introduction to the History of the Principal Kingdoms of Europe.* But whereas Pufendorf was aiming at a manual of modern history for young statesmen and government officials, Holberg wanted to create a more popular world history. His reworking of Pufendorf falls into three parts. He found Pufendorf's section on the history of the ancient world too meager, and he expanded it with the aid of a well-known Latin handbook. For the period

from the Middle Ages to the Treaty of Nijmegen in 1679 Pufendorf is his main source. After this he was writing contemporary
history. He deals with the events of the preceding thirty years
in considerable detail. Holberg's chapter on France, for instance,
fills seventy-six pages up until 1679, which is where Pufendorf
ceases, but French history from 1679 to 1708 occupies eighty-
five pages. Louis XIV's wars are described in great detail. At
least for the later years the sources must have been French and
German gazettes, so newspapers were once more the object of
his interest. It is significant that the originality of this book is
precisely Holberg's sense of what is topical, and he was never to
abandon completely the reading of newspapers. For instance,
when the *Introduction* was republished in a new edition in 1728
every chapter had been brought up to date. The history of France
had thus been expanded with a further twenty pages, and all
through Holberg's later works, his comedies, his epigrams, his
epics, his epistles, we find a sprinkling of topical references.
Some of the epistles were in fact written on subjects he had
read about in newspapers. And with this, his first, book, Holberg
wanted to cater for the newspaper-reading public. In it there
is all that a political tinker (cf. his later comedy) ought to know
about Prince Eugene and the Duc de Vendôme. And that is the
way that Holberg was to continue. He wrote no book without
a clear readership in mind. The object of any of his works was to
reach and gain readers.

When Holberg moved into Borchs Kollegium in August, 1709,
he felt he had achieved security. With his free lodging he also
received an annual sum of money. From the preface to the historical part of his *Introduction* it can be seen that Christian
Reitzer, Professor of Law, opened his library to him and encouraged him to write books of utility. So it seems plain that
Holberg's ambitions were centered on the University of Copenhagen. He wanted to qualify himself for a position with an
original historical work. So he set out to write a major volume
giving an account of the reigns of the Danish kings Christian IV
(1588–1648), Frederik III (1648–1670), and Christian V (1670–
1699). By the spring of 1711 he sent to the king an application,
which we know from a summary, for censors to be appointed
to pass a work he had completed called *Introduction to the*

History of the Last Three Most Rightful Kings of Denmark. The author was considering publishing it as a supplement to his original *Introduction*. Frederik Rostgaard was appointed to examine the manuscript, but the book did not appear, probably because the history of Christian V had not been completed.

About the year 1714 Holberg applied to the king for a professorship at the University of Copenhagen. In this application he testifies that he has composed a "continuation of recent Danish history." With this expression Holberg's intention becomes clear. In 1594–1603 Arild Huitfeldt, a Danish nobleman, had published *Chronicle of the Realm of Denmark*, which was reprinted in 1653. This work closed with the death of Christian III in 1559. Claus Christoffersen Lyschander had written the chronicle of Frederik II (1559–1588). This had long lain unprinted, but had finally been published in 1680 by Peder Hansen Resen. Lyschander's work had brought Danish history up to 1588, and Holberg intended to take up the story from there. It is interesting that Holberg's first scholarly project was to continue Huitfeldt and his successors and to make the history of the kingdom complete and of utility. Only about ten years after the death of Christian V he wanted to bring the history of Denmark up to date. We do not know definitely the state of the work in 1711 and 1714, but we have a good basis for judging. In 1729 Holberg published his *Description of Denmark and Norway*, and, as Chapter 6 in this work, he introduced, as he says, "the most distinguished part" of the manuscript that he had completed some years before on the reigns of Christian IV and Frederik III. He had also completed the history of Christian V, he goes on, and he would gladly have proceeded to the history of the reigning monarch, Frederik IV, if, as he expresses it, "His Majesty had not most graciously assigned to others the composition of such a history." Behind these words there undoubtedly lies a pang of regret. Andreas Hojer (of whom more later) had been given this task; his monograph *The Most Illustrious Life of King Frederik the Fourth* (in German) was not published until 1829. That Holberg thus squeezed his old manuscript into a book in which it did not belong was undoubtedly done so that he might prove to Hojer and the king that *the* historian of modern times was none other than himself, Ludvig Holberg.

Who could be better equipped to trace the events of the age than he? Who had read the newspapers more thoroughly?

If we look at the history of Christian IV and Frederik III as it has thus been preserved for us, we must admit that the author proceeded much more thoroughly here than in his popular work of history. The account given is extensively documented and moves forward with epic range and balance. If the history written in 1714 was indeed substantially the same as that which finally appeared in 1729 it would arouse considerable expectations for the author. This lost, and yet preserved, youthful writing earned Holberg admission to the rank of the scholars and to the university. In England a universal history had been the ambition of the young Holberg and had started him on a writing career. Now, in Borchs Kollegium, national history initiated him into scholarly research. History was thus Holberg's first important field of study. Like Pufendorf, he had a pragmatic conception of history; that is, he thought of history as being didactic. His was the old idea that history is made up of the collected experience of humanity. Throughout his life Holberg retained his historical view of phenomena—a chronological outlook. He wanted to look deeper than merely at the present state of things to discover their origin and root; he wanted to *voir venir les choses*, as more recent historians would say. Even in his youthful works we can observe how much pleasure Holberg found in making history set everything in its rightful place and bring order and progression to facts. Holberg could understand people and events when he saw them within a historical pattern. The historical outlook came to be a vital and lasting factor in Holberg's thought and understanding.

III *The Law of Nature and of Nations*

During the rich years of his twenties and thirties, however, Holberg also learned to look at matters from another point of view. This was through acquaintance with a field of knowledge that had been rejuvenated, or rather definitively established, in the previous century: natural law and the law of nations. It was probably Christian Reitzer, who was Professor of Law at Copenhagen University and lectured on this particular topic,

who proposed to Holberg that he should write an exposition in
Danish of this new and fundamental subject. From Borchs Kollegium it was only a few steps to Reitzer's residence, where,
as we have seen, a large library was at the young scholar's
disposal. Here Holberg worked out his *Introduction to the
Science of Natural Law and the Law of Nations* (1716). Holberg
was the kind of person who could learn for himself even while
he was writing for the benefit of others. In producing this handbook, which made a fashionable field of knowledge accessible
to Danish laymen, he acquired for himself a new mode of
thought: he amassed concepts and examples that he was to
remember throughout his life. Natural law and the law of nations
gave Holberg that systematic understanding of the world with
which theology and metaphysics were unable to furnish him.
Natural law was the kind of nonspeculative philosophy that he
could make use of. It also formed the gateway to the century
of the Enlightenment.

In the Epistle to the Romans St. Paul said that the Gentiles
have the Law of Moses written on their hearts. On the basis
of this, first Philip Melancthon and then later his Danish disciple
Niels Hemmingsen, an outstanding theologian and humanist,
maintained that the principles determining what was profitable
and unprofitable, what was honorable and dishonorable, might
well be found in the higher reason which God had implanted
in man, that is, in human nature itself. In 1625 Hugo Grotius
published his fundamental work *On the Law of War and Peace*;
in 1672 Samuel Pufendorf extended the scope of the system in
his lengthy work *On Natural Law and the Law of Nations*, followed in 1673 by an elegant pedagogical summary, *On the Duty
of Man and Citizen*. Pufendorf's most able pupil was Christian
Thomasius, whose *The Bases of Natural Law and the Law of
Nations Deduced from Reason* was published in 1705. All these
teachers of natural law were dominated by a belief in the
capacity of human reason to discriminate and to control, and in
his opening chapter Holberg states that it is our understanding that gives us light for our deeds; it can grasp and judge
what is evil and what is good, as long as it is not warped
to an unusual degree by an evil upbringing or evil habits. No
man should excuse the evil he does by saying that he under-

stood no better. It was this optimistic faith in human understanding that formed the basis of the Age of Enlightenment.
This comforting faith in human nature is scarcely so strong,
however, when Pufendorf seeks to explain how it is that human
beings have given up their original independent existence to
form societies. At this point Pufendorf is under the influence
of Thomas Hobbes, the consistent pessimist, who had come to
the conclusion, from his experience of the bloody English Civil
War, that only a strong state could hold human passions in check.
The power of the state must be like that monster described in the
Book of Job, to which "upon earth is not his like, who is made
without fear" (Job 41: 33). The name of this monster was given
by Hobbes as the title of his chief work *Leviathan*. In this book
the main argument is as follows: In the struggle of each against
all which obtained in the natural state, reason began to prevail,
so that men were prepared to sacrifice their liberty for the sake
of peace by agreeing to form communities. Thus, in learning
from Pufendorf, Holberg was also learning from Hobbes:

The true cause of communities and towns being established lies in
one man's fear of the evil of others, and for this reason the first human
beings yielded to law and authority, which were able to protect the
weak from the strong and to punish evil, which before that time had
abounded. If there were no law and justice, then, as the proverb runs,
one man would be able to swallow up another. Neither "Natural Law"
nor "Fear of God's Punishment" is sufficient to hold men in check.
(Part II, chapter 2.)

In this argument Holberg finds a justification for the absolute
royal power under which he grew up and which had given the
middle class, to which Holberg belonged, favorable conditions
at the expense of the deposed nobility and the downtrodden
peasantry. All his life Holberg remained a sincere supporter of
absolutism.

Holberg's *Natural Law and the Law of Nations* contains no
original thoughts, but it is inspired throughout by its author's
delight in discovery. Natural law became the secular philosophy
which could give answers to almost all the questions that a
citizen and a human being could ask. This basic work of Danish

enlightenment was finished in 1714, but it was not published until 1716. Before it appeared Holberg was to make an extensive journey in Europe, and how this came about will be related in the next chapter.

CHAPTER 3

Travels in the Latin World

I A Hasty Departure for Paris

ON January 29, 1714, Ludvig Holberg was appointed by the king to the unpaid post of *adjunctus professor philosophiæ*, which gave him the prospect of obtaining the next professorial chair to fall vacant. From then on his ambition was to obtain an established position within the University of Copenhagen. However, just at this juncture something unforeseen occurred. Since May, 1712, Holberg had been in receipt of a fairly generous scholarship, the Rosenkrantz stipend, of 120 rix-dollars per annum. This scholarship was tenable for four years, and an express stipulation was that the recipient was to spend at least three of these years abroad. Holberg plainly had no plans for travel. After all, he was receiving free lodging at Borchs Kollegium, and now that he could regard himself as a professor-to-be, there was no reason at all for him to leave Copenhagen. But Ivar Rosenkrantz, the sponsor of the scholarship, who was the Danish ambassador in London, was informed of Holberg's new appointment, and on March 23, 1714, a new candidate for the stipend appeared on the scene in the theological faculty. He had been awarded the scholarship "which had fallen vacant on Mr. Holberg's promotion." Thus Holberg found himself first appointed to an unpaid post and then deprived of his financial support. At this point he was advised by the trustee of the scholarship, Professor Hans Bartholin, to carry out its terms as quickly as possible and to travel abroad.

Holberg made all haste to depart. He sailed to Amsterdam and from there wrote to Professor Hans Gram that he intended to proceed to France and to stay some time there, or, as he expressed it, "until the vacancy arises." The idea of a permanent appointment was clearly still uppermost in his mind.

He deposited some of his effects in Amsterdam, so it would appear that he had no intention of remaining too long in Paris. In December the theological faculty adjudged that Holberg should continue to receive the scholarship. Holberg found it difficult to manage on the money in Paris and therefore moved on to Rome, where he had heard that the cost of living was lower. Altogether he remained two years in France and Italy, and during all that time impressions were crowding in upon him. Nowhere are his *Memoirs* more detailed or more vivid than when he is recounting his journey to Rome. It is a remarkable fact that Holberg was coerced into this journey, which was to change the direction both of his own intellectual development and ultimately of that of Denmark (indeed of Scandinavia).

Holberg traveled through Holland by horse-drawn barge. From Brussels he walked to Paris—a distance of some 300 kilometers, and when he arrived in the French capital he was footsore and weary. To begin with, he stayed in the smart tourist quarter around St. Germain des Prés, a center of the fashion trade and of theatrical life (Jean de France in the comedy he was later to write also stayed there). But Holberg could not afford to live there long; doubtless he had no money for going to the theater, at least he writes not a word about plays while he is in Paris. He soon moved on to the cheaper Latin Quarter around the Sorbonne.

The Paris Holberg had come to was the solidly Roman Catholic Paris of Louis XIV: great efforts were made to rescue Protestant souls. The newly arrived Holberg soon encountered some of his compatriots who had converted to Catholicism, and they sought to influence him. The leading proselytizer was Jakob Winsløw, a physician. He had been in Paris since 1698 and, influenced partly by Jacques-Bénigne Bossuet, had converted to Catholicism the following year. Bossuet was present at Winsløw's first Roman Catholic communion, and he instructed the priest to add the name Bénigne to Winsløw's baptismal name, so from that time forth Winsløw always called himself Jacques-Bénigne after Bossuet. Winsløw was an outstanding man of science; in 1721 he became a professor in the medical faculty in Paris, and in 1732 he published a textbook of anatomy which achieved a European reputation. He was pious by nature and an obliging personality who looked after his countrymen when they came to Paris. He helped Holberg to find his way around Paris, but in the spirit of Bossuet he tried to point out to him the great security to be found in the authority of the Roman Catholic Church. It was undoubtedly Winsløw too who sent Holberg to Saint-Sulpice, where Abbé Casset, a cleric of great debating skill, preached to heretics. He tried to provoke replies from them, and he was a master of the art of having the laughter on his side when his turn came to answer their objections. While Holberg was in Paris, Bernard Schnabel, a young Danish theologian, arrived there, and Holberg persuaded him to enter the lists with Casset and even to prolong his stay in Paris to attend a final debate.

It would seem that Holberg did not dare to advocate Lutheranism publicly himself, but he did so privately. In a large private library belonging to the Abbot of Bignon, Holberg felt very much at home, because the librarian was a Danish convert, Johannes Bormann. One day Bormann claimed that there was nothing Christian left to the Lutherans except the sacrament of baptism, and this sent Holberg into action. Just at that moment a French lawyer arrived and supported Bormann, and Holberg joined battle with arguments from church history. A German guidebook to Paris published in 1717 by J. C. Nemeitz warned travelers not to engage in religious controversy, but it would seem that this was unavoidable. Such intrusive attempts to convert were not without influence upon Holberg. He became fully aware of his Protestant convictions for the first time. Paris turned him into an anti-Catholic, and in this respect he was never to change his views. According to the terms of the Rosenkrantz stipend, Holberg was to study theology at Lutheran universities. He did not fulfill this condition, but paradoxically enough he spent much of his time thinking about religious matters, and his Protestant faith became established and militant. So his stay in France had the effect desired by the founder of the scholarship.

When we realize that in Paris Holberg was thus confirmed in his childhood faith, we can easily appreciate that he was not yet receptive to contemporary trends in biblical criticism, even though his curiosity about them had been aroused. In the great library, the Bibliotèque Mazarine, which was open to all, he saw the students lining up in the morning; when the library opened they would race in to borrow Pierre Bayle's *Dictionnaire historique et critique,* 1697 (*Historical and Critical Dictionary*), which expressed considerable doubts about the righteousness of God. Holberg does not say that he had the patience himself to read it, but later, when he reached Rome, he made attempts in two libraries to get hold of the book, but he was refused, for in Rome Bayle was a banned author. It was to be almost thirty years before Holberg concerned himself with the problems propounded by Bayle.

But what did Holberg read in the Bibliotèque Mazarine and in the other libraries he mentions? According to the rather sketchy information given in the *Memoirs,* he seems to have still been mainly occupied with history, both ancient and modern. In Paris, too, he seems to have made good use of his spare time. "To make the time pass," he writes, "I often went to the Palais de Justice to attend trials. I used to listen with admiration to the brilliant eloquence of the lawyers. They build up a speech with great skill, at one time playing on the chords of anger, at another on those of pity. It was like hearing Demosthenes or Cicero speaking French." Holberg also made trips into the environs of Paris, thus visiting Versailles (which he found even more magnificent than reputed).

II *On to Rome*

Something over a year after his first arrival in Paris, Holberg moved on to Rome, traveling both by river craft and on foot. Shortly after the death of Louis XIV on September 1, 1715, he passed through Lyon. Like his contemporaries he admired the fine buildings of the city. This city lost much of its splendor in 1793, when the revolutionary forces, enraged by its resistance, destroyed the mansions around the Place Bellecour. He moved on rapidly down the Rhone to Avignon and then on foot to Provence, fertile and populated country very much to Holberg's taste. He reached the Mediterranean at Marseilles, and the variegated world of the South opened up before his marveling

eyes. The French fleet of galleys manned by prisoners was lying
in Marseilles. "In this town," he writes, "I saw many unfamiliar
sights: people from the Orient and many galley slaves going
about the town with fetters on hand and foot.... It is a sight,"
he adds, "which arouses pity, but also a sort of joy, because
it is so unaccustomed." In Holberg's contemporaries compassion
is the strongest emotion. An Englishman, Edward Wright, who
saw the condition of the galley slaves in 1720 wrote that "it is
an amazing sight for an Englishman, and it provokes the strongest compassion, even though one is told that some of them have
committed crimes deserving of death."

During this journey Holberg was in peril several times. On
the way to Lyon his traveling companions turned out to be
scoundrels. In Genoa he fell ill with malaria, and on the crossing
to Civitavecchia, the port for Rome, his ship was menaced by
Algerian pirates. He does not conceal that he was frightened
then, nor later of snakes on the way from Civitavecchia to Rome,
but he forgot all these tribulations when he arrived and found
himself, as he says, "facing the greatest sight not only in Rome
but in the whole world: St. Peter's."

For Holberg Rome was primarily a city of architecture. He
read in the libraries about Roman antiquities so as to study
them later in the field. Thus for instance he visited the Colos-
seum; but ancient Rome did not fascinate him most—he was
taken up by the clear, restrained, and symmetrical lines of the
baroque. He had seen this style at Versailles, and in Rome
he praised Chiesa Nuova (which now stands in the Corso
Vittorio Emanuele). When on his way home he passed through
Turin, which as a fortress town had been extended on a rect-
angular plan, he called it the most beautiful city he had seen.

In Rome Holberg was not troubled by Roman Catholic mis-
sionaries, so he could easily follow the customs of the country
and bow to Pope Clement XI as he was borne about, and ascend
Scala Santa, the holy staircase, on his knees. In Catholic churches,
such as Chiesa Nuova, he heard sermons and concerts. Like
most foreigners he lived in the quarter around Piazza d'Espagna,
first of all with a French hotel keeper who suffered from a lung
disease and whose wife was a prostitute, and later with a
Piedmontese into whose house a troupe of Italian players moved

after Christmas—disturbing Holberg considerably with their noise. He was here encountering the *commedia dell'arte.* He relates in his *Memoirs* that about ten or twelve troupes of such players arrived in Rome at this time. Many years later, in Epistle 262, Holberg gave a vivid description of the multifarious life in the large square "called Piazza Navona, in which all kinds of merry spectacles are presented under the open sky. The Pope is unwilling to forbid such diversions to the Romans, and therefore allows them to continue, but so that it can be seen that he would rather condemn than approve them, he ordains that in the same place and at the same time as such merry spectacles are presented, a Jesuit is to make a speech at one end of the square, castigating such worldly merriments and follies. But people by the hundreds can be seen streaming to the amusements, whereas in general only one or two people approach the pulpit of the Jesuit."

III   *The Return Journey*

Holberg did not see the famous Spanish Steps—they were not built until 1721–25—but he ascended a more modest stair to the French conventual church of Trinità dei Monti, where he applied for treatment for an attack of fever. The French monks there carried on an excellent dispensary, where they issued free medicines to the poor. This dispensary was abandoned long ago, but the hall which housed it still exists: the ceiling is decorated with allegorical scenes. Holberg was so afflicted by the fever that on his journey back from Rome he had to ask for special dispensation from the rigors of Lent.

Toward the end of February, 1716, he began his long walk up through Italy: via Florence, Bologna, Turin to the Alps. He rode on a hinny up through the mountains and then whirled down into Savoy by sledge. He considered this country "ugly in appearance, twisted by mountains and rocks," but soon reconciled himself to it because it nevertheless had many villages and market towns. In Holberg's view beautiful countryside was land that was useful and cultivated. The great wild stretches of savage nature had no attraction to him. Holberg walked to Lyon, where he secured a place in a riverboat for Paris. But the evening before he was due to sail he was persuaded to drink heavily in an attempt to throw off his fever. When he was roused early the next morning he thought they were trying to rob him, and he screamed and shouted as if for dear life, and so did not catch the boat. He had paid for the ticket, so there was nothing for it but to walk the rest of the way to Paris. In Epistle 257 he tells us that a glass of wine, which makes others merry, makes him sad. *Il a le vin triste*, as the French say. How we have to admire the poetic imagination with which, in his comedy *Jeppe of the Hill*, he is able to depict to perfection inebriation in all its phases. Holberg had some money deposited in Paris and therefore could afford to take the mail coach to Amsterdam, but he had certainly done his fair share of walking —since leaving Brussels he had walked more than two thousand kilometers! In Amsterdam his fever left him, and he spent many hours making music with some friends. In good spirits he took ship to Hamburg and then continued overland to Copenhagen.

What did Holberg gain from his travels? He did not gather learning, nor did he assimilate the new and original ideas of his time. He probably saw very little of theatrical life and read little modern literature. But he had matured in many respects. He had seen France and Italy, thus broadening his horizon by becoming acquainted with Southern Europe as well as Northern Europe. He had rubbed shoulders with people of many kinds—not least common people, and his powers of observation had been made keener. His taste in architecture, both ecclesiastical and profane, had become established, and he had learned to understand and appreciate Italian music.

As soon as Holberg arrived home, he arranged for the publication of his *Introduction to Natural Law and the Law of Nations*, which had been printed during his absence. He wrote a preface to it, which not only gives a survey of the history of natural law but also, in a mature and authoritative way, outlines a program for modern studies and an evaluation of the current importance and usefulness of the sciences. He places first "moral philosophy, by which the mind is cultivated and a man is, as it were, fashioned, for this teaches us not only what is just and what is unjust, what is fitting and what is unbecoming, but also gives natural causes for these things." Among the useful sciences he places the science of medicine, then comes mathematics (which included mechanics), and finally historical inquiry, which is so exceedingly instructive. He considers the study of languages much overemphasized at the universities: "I cannot see," he continues, "how anyone can defend using his time in merely filling his head with a host of words." But worst of all are the logical exercises, teaching the young to "make black white and dupe ordinary people." Holberg is here thinking of the way young students were trained in abstract thought. They had to learn a series of abstract concepts, which together made up what was called metaphysics, and they had to practice the rules of logic. In 1713, in the geographical appendix to his *Kingdoms of Europe,* Holberg had already protested against the excessive importance given to these studies at the university, and it was one of Fortune's jests that after a long and uncomfortable period of waiting for a professorship, he was finally appointed Professor of Metaphysics. It is not surprising therefore that when, soon after his appointment, he delivered an oration in honor of metaphysics, it became, on his own admission, "more of a funeral oration than a eulogy." In 1720 another professorship fell vacant, and for the next ten years Holberg was Professor of Latin Oratory. His task was to expound the Latin poets. Remarkably enough, the beginning of his professional interest in Roman poetry coincided with his own breakthrough as a poet.

CHAPTER 4

A Poet Is Born

I The Eloquence of Anger

HOLBERG'S studies and interests up to 1719 would not suggest that he was going to turn into a literary figure. Even Holberg himself was amazed by the transformation. Everybody around him was versifying: the writing of occasional poetry was still a flourishing occupation, but he had no contribution to make there. He had read the Roman poets, but only for the sake of the language. And then suddenly he was seized by a poetic frenzy that was to last for five or six years! But Holberg is able to furnish a good explanation for his sudden discovery of literary talent. His anger made him wax eloquent when he felt his honor as a scholar impugned. He says that when he "sharpened his pen against satires" he "became a satirist" himself—first in Latin prose, later in verse. Satirical and comic writings were to fly from his pen.

The instrument of fate in this literary transformation was Andreas Hojer (1690–1739), a talented man from southern Jutland who had studied medicine, history, and law at Halle, and was at this time attempting to establish a career for himself in Copenhagen. In 1717 he competed unsuccessfully for a professorship in medicine. In 1718 he published in German a brief history of Denmark which described some of the Danish kings none too flatteringly. In the same year he published a Latin dissertation on marriage between close relatives. Arguing from natural law, he maintained that the usual objections to these unions could not stand up to scientific criticism. Both these writings brought their author reprimands from the highest quarters, but this had no effect on his career, for in 1722 Hojer was appointed royal historiographer. In this capacity he wrote

44

a history of Frederik IV, which we have already mentioned.
Hojer soon entered government service, achieved eminent positions, and proved to have a quick and sure grasp of affairs.
From 1734 until his early death he was also Professor of
Natural Law and the Law of Nations. Ever since the Reformation the University of Copenhagen had had professors of law,
but not until 1736 was an examination in law introduced. In
that year Hojer published a book dealing with the elements
of legal studies. It was written in Latin but was translated into
Danish in 1737. It is an interesting little book: it stressed the
importance of a lawyer's acquiring wide-ranging knowledge
and, above all, a broad humanistic outlook. Hojer possessed a
penetrating mind, a quick temper, and extreme ambition.

In the preface to his history of Denmark Hojer mentioned
Holberg's *Historical Introduction,* commenting that he had derived no benefit from it, because almost consistently it followed
Pufendorf. But in Holberg's book the chapter on Denmark
(which forms only about one ninth of the whole) is the most
original of all. In it Holberg is building directly on Saxo and
Huitfeldt. Hojer's remarks therefore cut Holberg to the quick,
and he turned upon him in fury. He did this in two short Latin
writings, *On Danish Historians* and *Concerning Marriage Between Close Relatives,* both of which appeared in 1719. They
are given the form of fictional disputations: the first is propounded and defended by two perpetual students well known
to everybody in the Latin Quarter of Copenhagen. In this
academic horseplay Holberg may have taken lessons from two
critical anniversary lectures which Professor Johann Burkhardt
Mencke had published in Leipzig in 1715 under the title
Two Addresses on the Charlatanism of the Learned. Solemnly
addressing himself to the *rector magnificus* and other worthy
auditors, Mencke gives numerous examples of the pedantic
niceties which occupy the minds of linguistic scholars, historians,
logicians, metaphysicians, mathematicians, and physicists. They
are not content with studying what can be observed on earth,
but try to find men on the moon, and hell and its devils on the
sun. Holberg similarly concludes his second disputation with
an imaginative characterization of Hojer as a polymath who
thinks he has mastered all the sciences. Holberg thus found

his wings in the polemical manner of Mencke. A passage like
the following, in which Holberg gives a pen portrait of Hojer's
failings, surpasses in eloquence anything he had written before.
His earliest characterization is a caricature. He finds himself
as an artist in these simple, direct lines translated here from
his Latin:

You are so eager to change things, so blind with ambition, that you
are ready to sacrifice your reputation, your honor, your life, your
welfare, so long as you can count as learned and brilliant. It
appears to me that you exchange one study for another merely so as
to wage war against the whole world of learning. Thus you follow in
the footsteps of Don Quixote, that knight of the sad countenance, who
recked not to challenge all giants wherever on earth they might be.
At one time you took the physicians under your treatment; more recently you attacked the historians with a superfluity of naughtiness;
and now finally even the greatest in the history of our fatherland.
And now you have turned upon the theologians and lawyers. Let the
mathematicians beware! For I hear there are preposterous rumors
about—such as that there are men on the sun or that the moon is made
of cheese, in any case nothing down-to-earth. . . . But we shall doubtless soon see you laying chains upon such men as Tycho Brahe,
Copernicus, Ole Rømer, and leading them in triumph. . . . Yes, I'll
give you some good advice: stop fighting with giants; cease from
challenging learned men, for a whippersnapper should not war against
giants but against cranes. In the words of Juvenal: you are but a foot
in stature against the men you so impudently and arrogantly try
to belittle!

Juvenal, whom Holberg here cites, is the most mordant of
the Roman satirists. Situations may arise, he says, so outrageous,
that even if nature has withheld from us the poetic gift, anger
itself will fashion the verse ("facit indignatio versum" Juvenal
I,79). Thus calumny can evoke art. After his polemical piece
about the marriage of close kin, Holberg attempted, as he put it,
a more bellicose style, and he wrote an imitation of Juvenal's
sixth satire, which deals with the corrupt morals of Roman
women. It took him several days to compose his first satire,
and a friend to whom he showed it judged that he was a poet
by nature, but lacked knowledge of versification. This was
the same criticism he had received as a schoolboy in Bergen

when he had teased one of the ladies of the house. His satire after Juvenal was first printed, doubtless after revision, in 1722, and in the meantime he had, as he says, with immoderate self-confidence written a great comic epic, *Peder Paars,* which appeared in 1719–20 under the pseudonym Hans Mickelsen. However, this work, which ushered in a new epoch in Danish letters, was not composed all at once but in stages.

II A Comic Epic

When he first launched into poetry Holberg sought inspiration in the great Romans. But later he turned to their French follower, Boileau (1636–1711). Boileau had composed a comic epic, *The Lectern,* which appeared in 1674–83. This describes how the clergy at Sainte-Chapelle in Paris were at loggerheads about the positioning of a lectern and the fierce battle which ensued. In subsequent editions of this book illustrations were provided, and after 1713 each canto was furnished with an engraving. Holberg's attention was caught by one of these showing the striving clerics in the heat of the final battle employing books as weapons. It was apparently this that gave Holberg an idea for a poem. This internecine strife over a trifle indulged in by the French ecclesiastics reminded him of the hairsplitting disputations and bigoted scholarship to be found in his own country. So he decided to write a satire set in the University of Copenhagen, the scene being a disputation, in which books came to serve as missiles upon the all-important question: Was Venus, in the Trojan War, wounded in the right hand, the left arm, or the thigh? In a footnote the poet remarks, "Examples of many quarrels of the same nature are found in Mencke's *The Charlatanism of the Learned.*" From Boileau then he borrows this scene as well as the goddess Discordia, who finds herself in her element in the University of Copenhagen. Holberg completed only this one episode and was then struck by another and brighter idea: to compose a long comic epic which, unlike Boileau's, would parody the characters and the action of Virgil's *Aeneid.* But when he was well on the way with this epic parody his thoughts returned to his original poem. He had no wish to waste a good composition, and although the battle of the books had not the slightest connection with the argument of his epic, he squeezed it into the story, revealing by a humorous footnote that he had twinges of conscience about doing so.

Both Antiquity and the Renaissance gave the epic pride of place. In Homer's *Iliad* and *Odyssey* the Greeks were able to relive the exploits of the past, and when Augustus was ruling over a Roman Empire at the zenith of its power, Virgil wrote his *Aeneid* dealing with the founding of Rome. An epic contains mighty events and the gods themselves participate in them. Thus three levels of will can be distinguished. The great heroes are able to determine their own deeds to a great extent, but they are powerless against the gods, who, in their turn, are subject to inexorable Fate. In the epic of Antiquity the will of Fate is usually understood as the decrees of the most powerful god, Zeus or Jupiter, or of the council of the gods. The epics of Homer and Virgil follow a similar pattern and are connected in argument. We may remind ourselves here of the argument.

It was strife between goddesses which led the Greeks off to Troy, which, after ten years' siege, they captured and sacked. On the side of the Greeks was Hera (in Virgil her Latin name is Juno), and on the side of the Trojans was Aphrodite (Venus). One of the surviving Trojans was Aeneas, whose mother was Venus herself and whose father was Anchises, a Trojan prince. And so, when Aeneas in the *Aeneid* of Virgil set out from razed Troy to found, according to the decree of Fate, a new Troy or Ilium on the coast of Italy, he was persecuted by Juno, who had no desire to see Troy resuscitated, but he was just as actively succored by his mother, Venus. When, after seven years' peregrinations, Aeneas set sail from Sicily, Juno persuaded Aeolus, the god of the winds, to raise a storm, which drove the Trojans across to Carthage on the north coast of Africa. Here Aeneas was cordially received by Queen Dido, whom Venus had imbued with a passion for the exotic Prince Aeneas. When Aeneas, obedient to the command of Destiny, was obliged to leave Dido, her love became so uncontrollable that she slew herself. When Aeneas arrived at the coast of Italy, the King of Latium promised him the hand of his daughter Lavinia, but her betrothed, Turnus, King of the Rutulians, was bitterly opposed, and not until Aeneas, assisted by Venus, had slain Turnus in single combat was he able to found Rome, whose imperial family could thus trace its descent from the goddess Venus.

Holberg had undoubtedly read Virgil while at the grammar school, and he knew his *Aeneid* very well. Scattered throughout Holberg's works are quotations from eleven of the twelve books of the *Aeneid*. But Holberg could evidently not appreciate the sacred solemnity which invests the epic narration. Not only in *Peder Paars* (III, 3), but several times later, he passed judgment that the Aeneas of Virgil was a cad who took unfair advantage of Dido only to abandon her on the feeble pretext that Venus had determined "another match" for him, thereby also robbing the noble Turnus of his betrothed as well as life and kingdom (*Moral Thoughts*, 472). Thus, to the solemn epic Holberg preferred romance, particularly satirical or humorous romance. As we have seen, too, Holberg had already compared Andreas Hojer to Don Quixote, and now, while mocking Prince Aeneas through the figure of the shopkeeper Peder Paars, he provides the latter with a companion, the down-to-earth scrivener Peder Ruus, who stands to Paars as Sancho Panza does to Don Quixote. And then the poet begins, following Boileau in selecting alexandrines in place of the hexameters of Homer and Virgil. We give the opening lines in the translation of Bergliot Stromsoe:

> I speak about a man whose exploits in life's channels
> Should justly be portrayed among the people's annals;
> I sing about a hero, worthy Peder Paars,
> Who on a journey went from Callundborg to Aars.

Like all parodies the poem about Peder Paars contains many-faceted comedy. It provokes laughter for gods to behave like ordinary mortals and for towering heroes to be replaced by middle-class nonentities. But the art reaches a higher plane when the gods and worthies of the parodist become figures in their own right and we forget the illustrious persons of whom they are caricatures. In *Peder Paars* there is a succession of comic characters and situations having their own independent value. From beneath the literary parody a powerful, earthy, almost primeval comedy emerges. We shall now trace the flow of this primitive comedy, which not infrequently develops a poetic diction of its own.

It is three years before the War of Kalmar, i.e., in 1608. Off Kalundborg is a vessel which Peder Paars has hired so that he can sail to Aarhus to visit his betrothed, Dorothea. So we are not in the Mediterranean but in Danish waters. Kalundborg is near the northwest corner of Zealand and Aarhus is on the eastern side of Jùtland. They are some fifty miles apart. A reunion of lovers, then, and obviously something to be prevented at all costs by the deformed goddess Envy. Off she goes to Aeolus to beseech him to raise a tempest: "O send a mighty wind and rouse the waves for me!" In the ensuing storm the calm and unruffled Paars and his scrivener address the sailors on the inevitability of death and inexorable fate, for "what fortune had decreed by none can be eluded." But they have to interrupt their lofty philosophical discourses because they feel seasick and need to vomit. Too late Venus, the protectress of all lovers, discovers the malicious deed of Envy. Paars and his craft are driven ashore, but "not a soul was lost." A man of extremely civil mien comes up to the shipwrecked party and he is able to tell them that they have been cast ashore on the island of Anholt, where the inhabitants had previously been very wicked, but now "improve from day to day in all respects." This kindly character describes vividly the self-seeking and arrogance of the authorities on the island, the bailiff, the priest, and the parish-clerk and at the same time he deftly picks Paars's pockets, stealing his purse. Later he brings up a band of natives who fall upon Paars and party, and after a fight, strip them to their shirts. But Paars remains so composed that even in such a plight he sets up a court martial to judge the ship's cook, who deserted during the battle. When sentence of death is to be carried out there is no priest to prepare the cook and so "a half-taught brigand" assumes the task of addressing words of consolation to the condemned man, but he prolongs his introductory remarks so excessively that the victim, who is kneeling, loses patience: "Alas, my knee is numb! That prologue is too long!" Then the executioner forgets to remove the sword from its sheath, so the cook escapes from the blow with his life, but they find it difficult to persuade him that he is not dead. During the night the shirts cause rumors of ghosts, and later the population of the island is terrified when Ruus breaks wind rather violently and the local wise woman, Gunild, thinks that the Turk has landed. However, Venus finally manages to do something to aid Paars: she implants a love for him in the heart of the bailiff's daughter Nille. As nobody knows what is wrong with the girl, Jens Blok, the barber, is called in, and he has reason to be proud of his skill as a physician:

> "To help Jens Jeppesen I hastened yesterday;
> He died 'tis true, but all his fever went away."

But he is of no help to Nille, and so Gunild has to come. The description of the old woman and her cat, who must both have something to eat before the consultation, is incomparable:

> "What happened?" she inquired when in the room she sat,
> Then begged some food be fetched for her and for her cat.
> So Martha kitchen-wench ran instantly with ardor
> To fetch these honored guests provisions from the larder.
> From off the servants' bread she cut a mighty piece
> And smeared on it nigh half a pound of poultry grease;
> She also poured some gruel in a lavish manner
> And placed it on a stool for tabby and his grammer.
> Our Gunild ate so fast the cat became quite wroth
> When none was left, and nearly bit her finger off.
> At once she boxed his ear as hard as she was able;
> The cat grew mild again and thus dissolved the squabble.
> Although the two from time to time would disagree
> They in a little while good friends again would be.
> But here in justice to the crone it should be noted:
> As though he were her husband on the cat she doted;
> Yes, from the very hour that Christen Smith she lost
> She loved no beast as well, no matter what the cost.

Meanwhile Jens Blok has discovered that Gunild is visiting the bailiff's house and there is a vigorous scene between the two medical rivals. The battle does not end until Blok seizes the cat by the tail and belabors the old woman with it. The sight of two crows, an ill omen, robs her of her fighting spirit and she flees. Another quotation from this part of the poem will show how literary parody is combined with humorous observation:

> Resplendent Phoebus stood a stone's throw from the ocean,
> And Thetis had prepared his porridge with devotion;
> The Nereids at once in all directions sped.
> One called out, "Deck the board!" Another, "Fix the bed!"
> The Tritons with the dinner plates came quickly springing
> To set the table while the evening bells were ringing.
> To make this matter more or less completely clear:
> The sun was setting and the evening drew anear
> When Gunild fled and tumbled headlong in the mire;
> Of Blok she thought not but reviled the crows with ire.
> She shrieked, "That evil sight has spoiled my victory;
> I else could have subdued my foe quite easily.
> If longer life be granted me by my Creator
> On those two crows I'll seek revenge a little later."
> Her tabby, that Achates faithful and so dear,
> Unhappily now scratched himself behind the ear;
> He made it known by wails more pitiful than ever,
> If they had stayed at home they would have fared far better.

The infatuated Nille now offers to assist Paars in leaving the island, intending to elope with him. But Venus exhorts Paars to be faithful to his Dorothea, and so he sails away without her and she is left wailing miserably at the faithlessness of her lover. They set sail for Aarhus, but Envy is once more on the rampage, and she persuades Morpheus to place himself on the steersman's nose. He then falls asleep and the ship ends up at Skagen, the northernmost tip of Jutland. After a brawl at an inn Paars and Ruus are dragged off to the town hall and later put in the lunatics' lockup. From there they are borne in procession out of the town. Don Quixote and Sancho Panza each take this in his own way:

> Thus with magnificence they marched in quick procession,
> But Peder Ruus who never had much self-possession
> Espied a pastry stall as on their way they sped
> And now he stopped to buy two twists of wheaten bread.

> Though by this deed my hero's heart was sorely riven,
> Like a philosopher he kept his anguish hidden
> And merely turned and to his scrivener softly said,
> "It is unseemly at this time to buy some bread."

Now their tribulations are almost over. Envy does indeed manage to make Niels Corporal enlist both Paars and Ruus as soldiers by an artifice, but from fear of the wrath of the mayor and citizenry he allows the two recruits to purchase their discharge:

> Thuswise his freedom was restored to Peder Paars
> Who, penniless, continued on his way to Aars.

And so we come to the end of this comic epic. The poet spares us the idyllic dullness of the lovers' reunion. *Peder Paars* extends to 6,249 lines of verse in fourteen cantos. It is one of the lengthiest attempts in literature at poetic and moral comedy.

III *Satires*

Holberg had started out on moral and social satire. *The Poet Advises His Old Friend Jens Larsen not to Marry* presents the same situation as Juvenal's sixth satire and Boileau's tenth. The Roman poet warned his friend against the appalling female sex, and the French poet reckoned up all the trials which a wife causes her husband. The Danish poet now adds the troubles brought by children small and large. Holberg, the eligible bachelor, does not allow marriage many advantages. His range is rather narrow in this satire on marriage, which was printed as number four in *Hans Mickelsen's Four Mocking Poems as well as Zille Hansdotter's Defense of Womankind* (1722). First in this collection of classical-style poems Holberg placed a universal satire, *Democritus and Heraclitus*, which had been printed separately in 1721. He was rightly proud of it. From Juvenal's tenth satire Holberg borrowed the two Greek philosophers, Heraclitus who wept at the folly of mankind, and Democritus who found it merely ludicrous. But on the basis of the contemporary conception of man, the satirist Holberg "proves" that men are to be both wept and laughed at, but mostly laughed at.

First he sketches the reasonable soul, the light that God has given us, and then the way our passions abuse this light. We are, as Boileau had emphasized in his eighth satire, worse than the beasts for they do not attack their own kind. Man is not only the most wicked, but also the most foolish of all creatures. Think of the oracles of the ancient Greeks and of the omens believed in, and now in our own time of the blind faith Catholics have in the Pope and of their teaching that the bread of the communion is transubstantiated into the body of God. "Ancient Rome was mad; modern Rome is no better." Looking around one finds fools everywhere; the world is a madhouse (verse 588). Among the fools Holberg names a man who behaves:

> Just as Tigellius, that estimated singer,
> Will never sing when men desire to hear his voice;
> When no man bids him, though, breaks forth in dulcet tones
> Till hearers are obliged to ask him to desist.

In *Apology for the Singer Tigellius,* the second satire of the collection, the capricious Tigellius, a character taken from the Satires of Horace (Book I, 2 & 3), is defended, it being pointed out that all men change their minds, nations and individuals go from one extreme to the other, we are only "constant in inconstancy" (verse 48). This is because there is a strange chaos in every man. In the third satire, *Critique of Peder Paars,* it is an easy task to defend a poet who castigates and ridicules. For if all are mad, the satirist can not be accused of aiming his shafts at particular targets.

The last poem in the collection differs from the others. It does not purport to be by Hans Mickelsen but to have been sent to him by Zille Hansdotter, who has composed it not in the masculine adagio of alexandrines, as the four satires, but in the shorter and more feminine *triple-tact.* In this long poem a learned maiden defends her gusto for reading. It is a result of prejudice and upbringing that women are regarded as unsuitable for study and other occupations reserved to men. The menfolk are afraid of women, and therefore they pretend that it is against nature for a woman to become a judge or an author.

If nature's distribution of gifts were strictly followed, many a statesman or officer would be set to watching the cradle.

Hans Mickelsen is given as the author of *Peder Paars*, of these satires, and soon after of the comedies. In the preface to *Peder Paars* he describes himself as "Brewer and Poet in Kalundborg." When Hans Mickelsen's poetical works are to be explained and defended, the author takes the more learned pseudonym of Just Justesen. In *Critique of Peder Paars* Hans Mickelsen himself defends satirical writings by referring to their utility. Wholesome satire resembles bitter medicine. Like a surgeon's knife it heals as it cuts (verses 211–212). But at the conclusion of the poem he appeals to an unnamed man whom he accounts the leading arbiter of taste in the land, and for this "Apollo in our land" poetry is neither learning nor utility, but art, imagination, mind . . .

> With marvel does one read great Homer's golden works,
> Imagination finds, not ancient Grecian wars . . .
> When France's name is praised, occur great names: Molière,
> Racine, Boileau, Corneille . . .
> One proves in learning rich, another *plein d'esprit*,
> One wise, sagacious is; one shows divinity.

This was the height Holberg had reached in 1722 in his understanding of literature as an art and in his understanding of himself. In the whole of this solemn tirade Holberg has his own *Peder Paars* in mind. The comedies are not yet in the picture. And yet it does shed a light upon Holberg's plays that in 1722 he had this lofty and liberal view of the art of literature, for it must have been in 1722 that Holberg was requested to write comedies.

CHAPTER 5

Comedies

HOLBERG is quite rightly known as the father of the Danish theater. We do not mean by this that there was no theater and no dramatic writing in Denmark before Holberg. By looking at what preceded Holberg's work we can best understand how his work renovated the whole of Danish culture.

I The Theater of the Middle Ages

The theater flourished in Europe during the Middle Ages. There were plays serious and plays lighthearted: the serious had subjects taken from the Bible or from the lives of the saints; the lighthearted were farces about laymen and clerics. Four plays in Danish have been preserved from Catholic times. There remain no dramatizations of the history of Christ or passion plays of the style still performed in Oberammergau, but we have a very powerful and vivid play, *Duke Canute the Saint*, which the clerics seem to have performed four times a year in Roskilde. The three others, two of which are broad farces, were presumably performed by grammar schools in Odense in the years just before the Reformation. Impecunious pupils had to act to maintain themselves at their studies.

II The School Theater of the Renaissance

After the Reformation it was once again the pupils of grammar schools who brought Danish drama before the public. This was the golden age of school drama, from about 1560 until 1630, under Frederik II and Christian IV. These two kings were very interested in the theater and had plays performed for them and their entourage at Copenhagen Castle or in various provincial town halls. For more ordinary people performances were held in the marketplaces and churchyards. Thus the theater of the Renaissance was not confined to the capital: on the contrary it developed most fruitfully in the provinces.

Everything depended on the rector, or principal, of the local grammar school. If he was interested in the theater and had poetic gifts, then his pupils would act plays that had often been written by the rector himself. Four Danish provincial towns succeeded one another as centers of such dramatic activity: Elsinore, Ribe, Viborg, Randers.

Obviously, saints could no longer be presented on the stage as they had been in Catholic times, but the most outstanding of the new plays were nevertheless of a religious character. No one ventured to introduce the person of Jesus Christ into the theater, but in Denmark as in the rest of the Lutheran world popular figures from the Old Testament were chosen, such as Susanna, Solomon, and Samson. In Ribe the rector, Peder Jensen Hegelund, translated a recent Latin play on the theme of Susanna, the honorable wife vilely accused by some concupiscent old men whose disgraceful advances she had spurned. The prophet Daniel exposes the two old men and they receive their condign punishment. There is no such clear morality in the play by Hieronymus Justesen Ranch, *Allegiance to Solomon,* which was a festive play ordered for the day in June, 1584, when Frederik II was to present his seven-year-old son Christian (later IV) to the people as heir to the throne at a court held in Viborg.

Ranch was the most gifted playwright within Danish school drama. At the same time as Shakespeare and a century before Molière he was producing an excellent comedy of character, *Stingy Miser.* The main character is a mean man who refuses his wife, family, and servants the necessities of life and finally leaves his home and dependents to manage without him. When he returns they all pretend not to recognize him, and at last, to the great satisfaction of the audience, he leaves his home once more in search of his wife, children, and property. The whole is presented in delightful Danish with brisk, earthy comedy and speech characterization.

III *Court Theater and Professional Troupes*

By about 1630 the best age of school theater was past. The clergy became more restrictive toward dramatic performances,

and this necessarily had an effect on schools. At the same time
the taste of the court was changing. People were no longer
satisfied with upright moral plays but wanted more visual
excitement and greater complication. A turning point was the
great feast in October, 1634, given by Christian IV on the
occasion of Prince Christian's marriage. Two mythological musical comedies were performed written by a professor at Sorø
Academy, Johannes Lauremberg. For the occasion a ballet was
also composed which included choruses and solos. In 1655
Lauremberg wrote a musical play (also in German) and in
1689 the first opera house was inaugurated in Copenhagen. It
burned down at the second performance, but a replacement
was built in 1703.

Thus during the establishment of absolute monarchy the
theater became an institution of some influence closely linked
with the court and Copenhagen, and the actors were no longer
amateurs but professionals. Wandering players had often visited
Denmark. As far back as 1585 we hear of English actors performing in Elsinore. But their German and Dutch imitators
became the most numerous, and after about 1660 Copenhagen
and the Danish provinces were regularly visited by German
and Dutch companies. In the 1660's Copenhagen even had its
first permanent theater—a large wooden building in which
various companies of players performed *Haupt- und Staatsaktionen,* which were equally popular with the common people
and the upper classes, in fact the players were often summoned
to play at court. These Dutch and German actors were among
the most renowned and the drama they presented was superb
in its own style. This was based on the traditions of the English
theater and relied on every kind of external effect. The subjects
were selected for the violent events they gave scope for on
the stage: the destruction of Jerusalem or of Troy, and the great
events of the century in Germany and England, such as the
histories of Wallenstein or Cromwell.

IV   *The Founding of the Danish Theater*

While this violent and noisy drama was flourishing, more
cultivated circles in Denmark began to acquire a taste for the

restrained and inward French style with its more natural performances of both serious and gay pieces. An early testimony to the influence of French literature exists in a dramatic satire from the time after the introduction of absolutism. A nobleman of ancient family, Mogens Skeel, in *The Comedy of the Count and the Baron*, borrows the pen of Molière in order to mock the new nobility which the absolute monarchy had established in 1671. On account of its political bias this caustic little comedy could, of course, not be staged or printed, but it was passed round and read clandestinely in manuscript. Under the theatrically-minded Frederik IV the court had both a French acting company and an opera company. Both the French plays and the Italian operas were performed at the new opera house until, about 1712, the actors moved over to the newly established stage in Copenhagen Castle. These artistic diversions were, of course, only for the upper crust; the masses had to be content with German spectaculars and low farce. But then a change occurred. A series of chance circumstances brought the drama of the upper classes into contact with that of the broad masses. A Danish theater was set up in which the new, valuable French drama was made accessible to all. Two Frenchmen were mainly responsible for this happening and thus, indirectly, for Holberg's comedies being written.

V *The Theater Is Founded*

At the royal Danish court there had been a French theatrical tradition. In 1721, after a break of some years, René Magnon de Montaigu was appointed to lead a complete troupe of court actors. He was an experienced man of the theater and through journeys to Paris was able to renew the repertoire continually. It seems clear that on occasion the public was admitted to these performances at Copenhagen Castle on payment of a fee. Holberg then, who does not seem to have seen any true plays in Paris, may have attended the excellent Copenhagen productions of Molière and his successors.

In 1721, however, the situation altered. The French troupe of actors had to give place to a German opera company and was therefore obliged to seek other employment. The entertainment world of Copenhagen was in the hands of Etienne Capion, a French émigré of great initiative who had been engaged in the tavern and victualing trade for many years. From 1713 he was also the scenery designer and manager of the court troupe. In 1719 he went into partnership with Salomon von Qvoten, a German theatrical manager, to present German plays in *Gethuset,* i.e., the cannon-casting works on the square called Kongens Nytorv. When J. C. Eckenberg "the strong man," a German tightrope walker, was becoming a fierce competitor, Capion secured him for his own theater. When Gethuset was no longer available, Capion had another quite new theater built and equipped in the same way as the theater in the castle. This lay in the street of Lille Grønnegade (now Ny Adelgade) and Montaigu and his troupe were engaged to play at this theater. On January 19, 1799, the theater opened with a performance of Molière's *L'Avare* and performances were then alternately in French and German. It soon became clear that Capion's undertaking was not profitable, and the French actors left the town, except for Montaigu, who on July 1, 1722, applied to the king for permission to produce plays in Danish.

It was a busy summer for Copenhageners interested in the theater. Montaigu knew that his application would be favorably received. The Royal Chancellor, U. A. Holstein, and Frederik Rostgaard, Chief Secretary of the Chancellery, were eager to promote the arts, and they were presumably responsible for a repertoire in Danish being made available. Some young clerks of justice were given the task of translating the French comedies that had been successful at court, and Professor Holberg, who was known as the author of *Peder Paars,* was requested to write something for the new stage. On August 14 Montaigu received his royal charter, and on September 23 the Danish theater opened in Capion's theater building with a performance of Molière's *L'Avare* in Danish translation. The very next performance, on September 25, was the première of a Danish original. This was *The Political Tinker* by Holberg. The theater maintained its momentum for the first few years, but then its success began to fade, and with varying fortunes it kept going until October, 1728, when a great fire, reducing large parts of Copenhagen to ashes, put a stop to all entertainments. In 1730

Frederik IV died, and Christian VI, who reigned 1730–46, regarded the theater as the work of the devil.

VI A Foreigner Goes to the Play

But before the theater had to close, Holberg managed to write about twenty-five comedies which he published, first in three volumes entitled *Comedies Written for the Newly Founded Danish Stage by Hans Mickelsen* (1723–25) and later he augmented this to five volumes called *The Danish Stage* (1731). By then most of them had been performed at the theater, alternating with translated comedies by Molière and other French dramatists, from whom Holberg learned much. In these years Holberg taught himself drama not only by reading but also by seeing his own and other plays on the stage. He lectured on Latin authors as part of his teaching duties at the university, and he had therefore studied the Roman comedians Plautus and Terence; the former in particular had considerable influence upon him. He found some inspiration in Aristophanes, the Greek comic genius with whom it all began.

One basis for evaluating Holberg's comedies is the use he makes of the European tradition of comedy. Another is the judgment of his contemporaries. A Swedish major general, Gustav Wilhelm Coyet, came to Copenhagen about the same time as the opening of the Danish theater in Lille Grønnegade. He tells us in his diary that he rarely neglected to attend "these Danish comedies, which pleased me very much both because of the skill of the actors and also because I found the Danish language particularly and subtly suited to comedy." He immediately procured the first two volumes of the comedies. He read them and "I must confess that while most comedies lose something of their force when they are read, these have retained if not augmented their effectiveness."

Right from the beginning, then, Holberg's comedies have been regarded as good reading. Among the most outstanding of them Coyet ranked *The Political Tinker, The Weathercock, Jean de France* and *The Lying-in Room* "as they contain pointed and profitable satire upon several common errors of everyday life." Coyet wrote this inside a Danish prison. In the winter

of 1722–23 he and a few consentient friends had hatched a
plot to bring the Faroes, Iceland, and Greenland under the
Tsar of Russia, and Norway under the Duke of Gottorp. This
dilettante plot was uncovered in February, 1723, and Coyet
had to remain incarcerated until his death in 1730. In prison
he wrote about the moral value of Holberg's comedies, among
them *The Political Tinker*. Presumably it did not occur to him
that he might have learned a great deal from this comedy. He
was an even greater visionary than Hermann the tinker. Coyet
was amused by the failings and weaknesses of his fellowmen,
and that is the solid basis of all moral comedies.

To understand a comedy by Holberg aright, we must view it
within the group of comedies to which its composition assigns
it. Five categories can be made: comedies of character; comedies
of intrigue; comedies of presentation; parodies; and comedies
of ideas.

VII *Comedies of Character*

The plays of Holberg had the same psychological background
as his works on natural law and as his satires. In most people
the light of reason burns but weakly: passions, whims, and
fixed ideas distort judgment. People are unbalanced, often ir-
remediably so.

When Holberg began to write comedies, he took Molière
as his most important model. Molière was the first to create
comedies of great value around the character of a single person.
Holberg, then, first exercised himself in comedies of character,
presenting a cavalcade of fools. But Holberg's comic fantasy
surpasses Molière's; he expands the characterization to its limits,
and there are glimpses of insanity in his best figures. The proto-
types of Holberg's great human caricatures are not in Molière's
L'Avare or *Tartuffe*, but in *Don Quixote*. Therefore Holberg's
comedies do not, like Molière's, call for psychological reflection
but for imaginative participation. Holberg transforms classical
comedy into sublime farce. He was able to find yet other human
types and to place them in actions which expose their foibles
to laughter. Each of them stands in his natural milieu, but they
are out of harmony with it because they have pretensions un-

suited to their station or they boast of abilities they lack. Together they present a gallery of fools having validity in all ages.

We will look first at *The Political Thinker,* the self-confident politician who does not know what he is talking about. This is one of Holberg's most brilliant plays; it is traditional to place it first, and therefore fitting that we should deal with it first here. Holberg himself placed it first in both the collections of comedies (1723 and 1731) which he published. With this comedy the reader is placed right back at the beginning of the eighteenth century, when the middle classes all over Europe were just starting to form political opinions, without, however, having sufficient basis of knowledge. Some of this knowledge was to be provided for them by Holberg's didactic works, e.g., his *Introduction to the History of Europe* and *Description of Denmark and Norway.* Both *The Political Tinker* and *Jeppe of the Hill* are variants of an old tale about the simple man who is elevated to be a ruler for a single day. Both of them have an anti-democratic tenor: when beggars are raised to sit with princes, they do not know what to do. The dramatic centers of gravity in *The Political Tinker* are in Act 2, in which Hermann and the other ignorant artisans outdo one another in political visions, and Act 5 with its brilliant counterpoint of the tinker, who has been made to believe he is mayor of Hamburg, and his servant, Henrik, who is the victim of the same illusion but, with a grain of common sense, wishes to exploit the situation to his own advantage.

The plot in *Jeppe of the Hill* goes back to an anecdote in a fictitious travel memoir *Utopia* (1640) by the German Jesuit Jacob Bidermann. With conscious artistry and great dramatic skill Holberg elaborates on Bidermann's simple comedy. Holberg makes Jeppe's wife so shrewish that this explains why he drinks. But Holberg also makes him a cowardly and therefore ridiculous husband, henpecked and cuckolded. Jeppe excuses his propensity for liquor by referring to his downtrodden position and thereby, to the unsentimental eyes of Holberg's age, becomes even more of a joke. And finally Holberg makes Jeppe a "man of wit." At the castle, when Jeppe finally believes that he is a baron, he becomes a worthy comrade and opponent in this distinguished company. He knows how to hold his own and this is what makes the repartee in these scenes so amusing. And yet Jeppe's lucid moments make him even more ridiculous, for from his correct premises he draws incorrect, indeed perilous, conclusions. As a copyholder he knows how a bailiff makes money by defrauding his employer, but, for this, as a baron, he is prepared to have not only the bailiff but also his seven children hanged! The coward of Act 1 is a suitable candidate to be a tyrant in Act 2. It is a happy relief for the spectators to see him once more on his dunghill. The dramatist intends everything about "the transformed peasant" (the subtitle of the play) to make respectable people laugh.

In his satirical poem about the singer Tigellius, Holberg had tried to prove that all of us, men and women, are fickle. In *The Weathercock* the changeable character is a woman, so Holberg can form the comedy into a game in which three men face one widow. The suitors are, of course, fools, but only of the second rank. The capricious Lucretia manifests her greater insanity right to the bitter-sweet end. Two of the men find their way back to their true betrothed, and she gives her hand to the third. Then she suddenly changes her mind and leaves her learned admirer high and dry. The hilarious point of insane release comes in *The Fussy Man* when the title character, Vielgeschrey, discovers that he has been made a fool of. He then leaps up from his chair shouting that he is Alexander the Great and they shall all die by his hand.

It is part of the comic irony for the crazy main character to be exposed to our laughter when he or she is confronted with people who are inferior in social rank or intelligence. In a great comedy of character entitled *Erasmus Montanus, or Rasmus Berg*, Holberg gives a penetrating and comic portrait of a bogus man of learning. A kindly and well-to-do peasant family is visited by their son, Rasmus Berg, whom they have sent to the capital to study. The young man has not been slow to Latinize his name according to the custom of the learned men of his time, and his one passion is to carry on disputations in Latin for the pure pleasure of disputation. For him learning is something purely formal: a learned man is a man who can prove all his statements by the magic of syllogism.

Montanus. . . . I can dispute in good Latin about any subject you like to mention. If someone says that this table is a candlestick, I will defend that statement. If someone says that meat or bread is straw, I will defend that, too. I have done so many a time. Listen, Father, do you think that a man who drinks well is blessed?

Jeppe. I should rather think that he was accursed, for he may drink his good sense and his money away.

Montanus. I shall now prove that he is blessed. Quicumque bene bibit, bene dormit. . . . No, of course, you don't understand Latin, I shall have to say it in Danish: He who drinks well usually sleeps well. Isn't that so?

Jeppe. That's true enough. When I'm halfway to getting tight, then I sleep like a horse.

Montanus. He who sleeps soundly, does not sin. Isn't that true, too?

Jeppe. Yes, that's true enough. As long as you're asleep, you don't sin.

Montanus. Blessed is he who sins not.

Jeppe. That's true, too.

Montanus. Ergo, blessed is he who drinks well. Mother, I am going to turn you into a stone.

Nille. Hark at him. I'd like to hear him do that.

Montanus. All right, now you shall hear. A stone cannot fly.

Nille. No, that's right enough—except when someone throws it.

Montanus. You cannot fly.

Nille. That's true, too.

Montanus. Ergo, mother is a stone.

(*Nille starts to cry*)

Montanus. Why are you crying, mother?

Nille. Oh, I'm so afraid of turning into a stone; my legs are beginning to get quite cold already.

Montanus. Cheer up, mother. I'll make you into a human being at once. A stone cannot think or speak.

Nille. That's true. I don't know if it can do any thinking, but it certainly can't talk.

Montanus. Mother can speak.

Nille. Yes, thank God, I can talk—like a poor farmer's wife.

Montanus. Good, so ergo, mother is not a stone.

Nille. Ah, that made me feel better; I'm coming around again now. Good gracious, you certainly need a strong head to study. I don't know how your brain can stand it all. Jacob, from now on you must be at hand to help your brother; there's nothing else for you to do.

(Act II, Scene 3.)

Further on, Erasmus declares to his brother that he has no wish to be dragged into a dispute with "the kind of peasant-scoundrel that you are. If you understood Latin, I should be able to give you satisfaction at once. I am not practiced in disputing in Danish."

Jacob. You mean to say, mounseer, that you've got so learned that you can't explain what you mean in your own language any more. . . . But the little bit I understand is the sort of thing that everybody can understand when I tell them.

Montanus. Oh, yes, you are a learned fellow, all right. Tell me what you know.

Jacob. Supposing I could prove that I was more learned than you are, mounseer?

Montanus. I should certainly like to hear you do that.

Jacob. In my opinion, it's the man who studies the most important matters that has the deepest knowledge.

Montanus. That is true enough.

Jacob. I study farming and the tilling of the soil, so therefore I am more learned than you are, mounseer.

Montanus. So you think rough peasant's work is the most important?

Jacob. I don't know. But I do know this, that if the farm workers were to take pens and pieces of chalk in their hands and start measuring how far it is to the moon, then you learned men would soon start to feel it in your bellies. You scholars spend your time disputing whether the world is round, four-sided or eight-sided. And we study how to keep the land in good order. Can't you see, mounseer, that our studying is more useful and more important than yours, and that therefore Niels Christensen is the most learned man in this village, because he has improved his land so much that it yields thirty rix-dollars worth more an acre than it did when the last man had it, who spent all day with a pipe of tobacco in his mouth, smudging and dog-earing Huidtfeldt's chronicle or some book of sermons.

Montanus. This will be the death of me. It's plainly some devil speaking. I have never in all my life thought to hear such words from the lips of a farmer's boy. For although all you have said is false and ungodly, it was an uncommon good speech for one of your station. Tell me from whom you have learned to spout such nonsense?

Jacob. I haven't done any studying, mounseer. But folks say I've got a good head. The judge never comes to this village without sending for me right away. He has told my parents a hundred times that they ought to keep me to my books, and that I might get somewhere. When I've got nothing to do, then I start speculating. The other day I made up a verse about Morten Nielsen, who drank himself to death.

Montanus. Let me hear the verse.

Jacob. First of all, you've got to know that this man Morten's father and grandfather were both fishermen and got drowned at sea. The verse went like this:

> Here doth Morten Nielsen lie,
> Who to follow the footsteps of his family,
> Who as fishermen died at sea,
> Drowned himself in brandy.   (Act IV, Scene 4)

According to Holberg's preface to the first volume of his comedies, *Erasmus Montanus* was complete in 1723. It was first printed in 1731, but was not performed until 1747. It is a comedy that has continued to rise in esteem not only as a play for acting but also for reading. There can scarcely be any other play in the world to expose useless knowledge with such genius as this. It often operates as the scholar's bad conscience if he has a feeling that his employment of scholarly methods is stifling his interest in the material he is working with. In this comedy Holberg criticized the university exercises of his day in formal logic, i.e., a particular part of university education. It is instructive to see Holberg stating elsewhere precisely what he had against the system. This is to be found in Holberg's oration after he had been made rector of the university in 1735–36. In this oration, Holberg maintains that logical disputations have value only for budding lawyers and it is therefore wrong to distribute degrees and stipends to students of all subjects according to their skill in disputing. A theologian should be tested by his sermons and commentaries, a medical student by his observations, a physicist and philosopher by his ability to present the most probable hypotheses, and a mathematician by his ability to prove propositions. Only legal tests should be disputations, as it is only in court that such methods have their uses. The whole of this speech bears witness to Holberg's sound and mature view of higher studies.

Jean de France, whose protagonist is Hans Frandsen, the son of a Copenhagen burgher, is just as full of French affectations as Montanus is of Latin. His servant, though following his master through thick and thin, nevertheless takes the opportunity of making fun of him.

Jacob von Thyboe, which was performed and printed for the first time in 1725, is a beautiful example of how a dramatic poet can adopt figures, situations, and dialogue from older literature and nevertheless be dazzlingly original. In Act 2 of this play Holberg has written a scene from Plautus's comedy *Miles Gloriosus.* The Roman author shows us the vainglorious officer making himself important with imagined exploits, and his companion Jesper Oldfux, who flatters him shamelessly in order to secure for himself good food at the officer's expense. The swaggering warrior believes he is as brave in war as he is irresistible in the eyes of women. The flatterer keeps account of the thousands the boaster has slain and confides to him that many women are begging to be allowed to approach him, for he is so handsome. Holberg succeeds in moving these two characters to Copenhagen. In Holberg's time Jutlanders were regarded as boastful people who could tell tall tales with aplomb. Thyboe's military language is German, of which, too, Jeppe of the Hill had learned a little while he was in the army. Jesper Oldfux is a teasing, cheeky Copenhagener who mocks the stupid officer at the same time as he flatters his vanity. In Holberg's comedy, then, the two comic types still exist on their own. In a comedy written in 1844, *The Neighbors,* Jens Christian Hostrup, one of Holberg's most talented successors, combines the boastful soldier and the parasite into one person. These figures of comedy live and change in this way: there is about 2,000 years between Plautus and Hostrup.

Holberg is past master at such scenes. The secondary characters strike sparks off the fool in their midst and at the same time characterize themselves. In *Gert Westphaler* this interplay fails because the barber's particular weakness is to talk only of himself. This play has therefore never been a success on the stage.

In a couple of comedies the interplay rests on a rather harsh type of comic effect which is little to the taste of modern audiences. We realize that we are in an age when compassion is a scarce commodity. For the maid in *The Fortunate Shipwreck* can say of the undeniably not very attractive Rosiflengius in his hearing that "he must have got just as much of a hump in his brain as on his back." At the home of the highly distinguished but impoverished Don Ranudo a rotten chair collapses and his spouse, Donna Olympia, falls onto the floor so that her guest notices that her clothes are ripped and ragged at the back. In such situations Holberg's comedy is merciless. *The Fortunate Shipwreck* presents two human types. Up to Act 4 we are shown the professional poet, whose laudations are available to anyone who can and will pay for them. From that point on, the moral poet, Philemon, occupies the main place on the stage. He tells people the truth in verse and in prose and is the dramatist's hero and mouthpiece. Thus the comedy falls into two parts, of which the first is intended to show bad praise, the second good, i.e., justified, criticism. *The Fortunate Shipwreck* may be regarded as an expression of the rational and moral intention of the comedies. *Don Ranudo de Colibrados or Poverty and Pride* is not a protest against nobility and rank. The play is a ruthless demonstration that it is against all common sense—and therefore ridiculous—to cherish such a pride of station when one has no financial basis for living up to it.

In 1728, when Holberg published a new and enlarged edition of his manual of natural law, he inserted in the chapter on good name and reputation, a passage in which he distinguished between two kinds of people of rank: those whom the authorities of their own volition have raised to eminence, thus declaring them to be of a higher quality than their fellow citizens, and those who have attained their rank by constant and persistent pestering of the authorities for it. In Holberg's words, "When a citizen without especial merits seeks advantages above his fellow citizens, who are just as good as he, he then manifests his pride and frailty and thus, as it were, declares himself more imperfect than others." Thus in the comedy *Social Ambition,* Holberg can convincingly ridicule a rank-seeking worthy who tries to barter his way to position and title. And with the same good conscience, some twenty years later, when with his pen and through other means he had acquired two manor houses, Holberg can permit himself to be raised to a barony. By then Holberg had the means that Don Ranudo lacked and, as he was unmarried and childless, he gave them back to the community (see Chapter 10). He then felt that he had merited the regard and esteem that accompanied the dignity of a barony.

He also felt a profound satisfaction at the circumstance that a Scandinavian man of letters could achieve a place in the nobility, thus emulating the German philosopher Christian Wolff, who had shortly before (in 1745) been made a Baron of the Empire.

The comedies of character are Holberg's most precious gift to the Danish theater. Generation after generation has read them afresh. There have been many new productions and new interpretations. They have the profound nature of genuine poetical works, which means that different ages make them the vehicle for their best efforts, so that even completely wrong interpretations still have value.

VIII   *Comedies of Intrigue*

When Holberg wrote character comedies he was trying to find human types which other comedy writers had not already worn out by use. Each character comedy has its own main character. The subsidiary characters may recur in play after play, for instance, the servant Henrik and the maid Pernille. But Holberg also wrote another kind of comedy without a defining main character in which the same stock characters are found again and again: the querulous old man, the young people in love, the servants, etc. The same people seem to be acting different plays. And in a way this is the impression intended. For centuries in Italy there had been a special form of comedy, *commedia dell'arte,* masked comedy in which each actor in the troupe always represented the same figure—the captain, the doctor, Harlequin, Columbine—and these actors performed a number of slight comedies that differed only in plot. The characters were always the same, but the intrigue varied. It was like a game using the same pieces to make an infinite number of combinations. The Italians came to France, where they played in both Italian and French. Their plays were published and Holberg borrowed very much from them, and not only for his comedies of intrigue. In some there are servants who produce complications or are themselves caught up in them: *Pernille's Short Ladyship, Henrik and Pernille,* and *The Invisible Lovers.* In others, the intrigue rests on a misunderstanding of which all the characters are victims: *Without Head or Tail, Witchcraft or False Alarm.*

The background to the intrigue in *Pernille's Short Ladyship* is the almost unbridgeable gulf which in Holberg's century separated the servant class and those they served. In this comedy an old widower, Jeronimus, attempts to grab the rich heiress whom his stepson loves, but a trick is played on the old gentleman so that he is married off to the serving maid— and for her it is the height of good fortune to leap from her station as a servant to that of lady of the house, even though this requires being married to an old curmudgeon of a husband.

In *Henrik and Pernille*, as well as in *The Invisible Lovers* (i.e., the masked lovers), the comedy of mistaken identity is played in the Italian style. In both plays Holberg succeeds in juxtaposing with skill and contrast the amorous enmeshments of the young gentry and the more straightforward foils of the servants in love. In *Henrik and Pernille* the intrigue also springs from the social setup. A servant dons his master's clothes and becomes acquainted with a grandly dressed lady, pays court to her and is well received—but this woman is a lady's maid dressed up in her mistress's clothes! And each of these two grand young people, who become betrothed, comes to suspect that the other has plighted his troth to someone else! This gives rise to lively and good situation comedy, as it does in *The Invisible Lovers*, in which the servant apes his master in love affairs. When the master, in spite of being betrothed, falls madly in love with a lady whose face he has never seen, because she is hiding behind a mask, the servant casts off his unpretentious and willing girl friend and serenades a masked lady. Fortunately, the master's masked mistress proves identical with his fiancée, and, on hard conditions, the servant is forgiven by his plebeian girl friend.

In two very independent comedies Holberg makes superstition the cause of Italian misunderstandings: *Without Head or Tail* and *Witchcraft or False Alarm*. *Without Head or Tail* bases its comedy on a clearly psychological theme. In his autobiography Holberg summarized its content as follows: "The main characters are two brothers, of whom one is superstitious, the other incredulous. However, when a friend attempts to cure the faults of each, the superstition of the one degenerates into incredulity and the incredulity of the other degenerates into superstition.

Thus the comedy demonstrates that any error consists in going to excess and that reforming zeal drives itself so far that we slide into the opposite extreme." A parallel, though not a source, to this comedy is found in the following story which Leibniz liked to relate: Of two brothers one had become a Catholic and tried to convert the other, while the latter was just as eager to win back his brother to Protestantism. The result was that each convinced the other—and the final conclusion was that, because of their great zeal, God had mercy on both!

Witchcraft or False Alarm finds its theme in the final phase of the persecution of witches in Denmark, and reading it can still give us a shudder as in Arthur Miller's *The Crucible*, but in Holberg's hands the play is nothing but sport. For the dramatist this comedy of witchcraft is a merry rout: it amuses him to create a rumor that arises and spreads and grows continually. The victims of the rumor are a group of actors who, in a small Danish town, are accused of witchcraft; these are also the heroes of the comedy. The story revolves around the illusion mongers, first of all the leader, who is called Leander. For Holberg he is undoubtedly a kind of Harlequin, the transformation artist from the Italian theater of improvisation, the *commedia dell'arte*, to which reference is made in several places. It is an Italian comedy right to the final effects, which form the most brilliant of Holberg's "oblique" conclusions. A trial has been held, the innocence of the actors established and the judge has departed, when two women come rushing in—the mother of one of the actors and the wife of another. They do not know the outcome of the case and therefore overwhelm the clerk of the court with prayers for help. After all, the accused "is a young man and he might easily be led astray, let him at least be buried in consecrated ground."

Diderich the Terrible, which is set in Venice, is Italian in a different sense. Holberg here makes use of two comedies by Plautus, *Pseudolus* and *Curculio,* and transferred the action to a more modern European war in which Venice played a part that was well-known in Denmark and Norway. We recall that in his young days Holberg's father had been an officer in Venetian service. The title figure of the play is a boastful officer who buys a girl prisoner of war and wants to make her his mistress, but by a robust intrigue he is given his own wife instead, and the soldier who had recently been boasting of his prowess has to submit ignominiously to a beating from a woman!

IX   *Comedies of Presentation*

Between the pure character comedy and the comedy of intrigue lie a number of plays which have as their particular task the presentation on the stage of a custom or festivity which the audience know from their own experience. Such comedies are *The Lying-in Room, The Christmas Party,* and *Masquerade.* Therefore this group can be called presentation comedies. They are like *tableaux vivants* with many walk-on parts. In *Journey to the Spring* even the journey itself to the healing spring is presented on stage as well as the gay life found there. Such dramatic entertainments were very popular.

Following an Italian model, Molière once wrote a bright little comedy (*Les Fâcheux*) in which a marquis in love is scarcely able to speak to his beloved because one troublesome person after another appears to claim his attention. One of Molière's pupils, Boursault, wrote a similar play called *La comédie sans titre* in which a dozen people come on the stage at the house of the pretended editor of a fashionable monthly paper *Le Mercure Galant* and pester him to whitewash them or publicize them in his paper. This latter play gave Holberg the idea and even more for the great act in *The Lying-in Room* in which the ladies who come visiting are practically the death of the poor woman. Holberg understood beautifully how to exploit this genre, which is called *pièce à tiroirs* and which gives a long series of actors an opportunity to show off their abilities each in a small but vivid role.

The Lying-in Room is almost two comedies in one. There is first the comedy of the aged husband who, unjustly, fears that he is not the father of the child. In Act 1 Holberg is well on his way to writing a comedy of character about an "imaginary cuckold." Corfitz, the confused master of the house, is given a servant named Troels who at one and the same time supports him and increases his disquiet. This stupid, yet cunning, servant is among the best characters in Holberg. We are preparing to watch this relationship between master and servant develop along the lines of that in *The Political Tinker* and *Masquerade*. But Act 2 brings us into a comedy of a completely different kind. Corfitz, who dominated the whole of Act 1, is now no longer the main character—he disappears under the table and women monopolize the stage. A stream of females come to pay their respects to the young and attractive mother.

Holberg's idea in this scene did not only live in his own comedy but also caught on in others. "Why does no one write a literary *Lying-in Room*," remarked Søren Kierkegaard in his book *Preface* (1844). "Literary people bear a striking resemblance to the ladies in that comedy—people who kill the unfortunate person with chatter; envious, malicious people who have tongues worse than those of such ladies." Hans Christian Andersen seized hold of Kierkegaard's idea and in 1845 he had success with *The New Lying-in Room*. It is a feature of this genre that it can be shortened or lengthened according to the requirements of the theater. Holberg made big changes in *The Lying-in Room* between the first edition of 1724 and the second of 1731. It is therefore legitimate to do as the Royal Theater in Copenhagen still does and omit the scenes with the doctors, even though these do possess a certain comic attraction.

From the lying-in room itself we finally return to the comedy of cuckoldry in the final scene. The self-induced worries and doubts of old Corfitz are multiplying until he suddenly realizes that he has been unjust to his young wife. And then he expresses himself thus: "I will go in and fall on my knees before my wife, kiss her hands and beg with tears for forgiveness." Here, as in other comedies, Holberg devotes himself with relish to farce and its exaggeration, but he still retains small human touches.

Even in the first months of the new theater Montaigu was performing lavish costume pieces and *comédies-ballets* by Molière such as *Monsieur de Pourceaugnac* and *Le Sicilien*. The audience wanted something to look at. Now the stage had yet another house playwright beside Holberg. This man was Joachim Richard Paulli (1691–1759). In 1723 he had produced and published a comedy in three long-drawn-out and clumsy acts, *The Blindness of the Sighted*. In the same year the theater seemingly requested him to write a festive piece which came to be called

The Christmas Party and Masquerade, and this was printed in 1724. The actors evidently felt that in spite of some lively details the construction of this comedy was much too ponderous, and they asked Holberg to look over the manuscript. With his sense for dramatic proportions, Holberg divided Paulli's play into two *divertissements*: kickshaws built around seasonable games and a masked ball, respectively. Holberg did not borrow very much from Paulli's clumsy intrigue, but he did adopt a few touches in *The Christmas Party* and in *Masquerade.*

In *The Christmas Party,* the Yuletide festivities, extensions of heathen saturnalia, give the old-fashioned paterfamilias Jeronimus occasion for concern. But when he wishes to deny his household a Christmas party, he has them all against him: not only his young wife, who is awaiting a tryst with a young gentleman of the neighborhood, but also his own sister, who asserts that the neighbors will think that the family has lost its Christian faith and will regard them as Turks and heathens. But the decisive defense of the festivities is provided by the children's tutor. His speech is a wonderful example of comic logic: "*Just as* the bird Phoenix, which is found in Arabia, lives for a thousand years in solitude and burns herself up as soon as she produces a young one so that she shall not live in society or intercourse with others of her kind, *so* ought we human beings, *on the contrary,* in order to demonstrate that we have no kinship with such a dumb creature, be sociable and hold festivities." Jeronimus then admits defeat: "The parable of the bird Phoenix struck me very forcibly." And Pernille, the serving maid, exults, "Oh, that lovely Phoenix bird, all other birds are only rabble compared to it!"

In *Masquerade,* too, Holberg shows his ability to vary the comic effect so that it also gives capable actors some splendid opportunities. A father has selected a suitable marriage partner for his son, but the young people have not yet seen each other. At a public ball the son becomes infatuated with a young lady and exchanges rings with her. The faithful servant wants to show his master what this can lead to, and quite alone he performs a little comedy in three acts, in which the father, the son, the father-in-law, the intended bride as well as lawyers and a judge each have their several speeches. This is justifiably a sought-after virtuoso part for Danish and Norwegian actors. Of course Holberg is obedient to the rules of comedy and sees to it that the lady from the masquerade ball and the betrothed are one and the same girl.

In some scenes in *Journey to the Spring* Holberg employs parody effects. He was no lover of opera, which seemed to him an unnatural art form. In *Journey to the Spring*, when the father has betrothed his daughter against her will, the young girl makes out that she can only express herself in song. Two false physicians —the favored adorer and his servant—advise a visit to a miracle-working spring outside Copenhagen. The audience is then treated to singing in both German and Danish before the two young people run away and then are overtaken. And then it is said of the maiden: "She sings no more, she weeps"—until a happy conclusion is provided for this journey to the spring.

The Eleventh of June, the half-yearly settlement day, when creditors came to the capital to claim interest on loans, was a welcome opportunity for the theater to show the public, including the esteemed capitalists, the stock exchange and the life that went on there. At the same time this play is a vigorous comedy with a tricky man of wealth who comes from Jutland to fleece the Copenhageners, but comes in for some rough treatment himself before, left only in his shirt, he has to leave the capital. The more sharp-witted cheat the less wise.

There is also coarse rough and tumble in the two thorough-going comedies of rascals, *The Peasant in Pawn* and *The Arabian Powder*. In the former an indebted fortune hunter exploits a simple country bumpkin sent to the city to buy tar, in order to lay hands on valuable goods. The peasant is presented as a Count Palatine, and the trickster as his majordomo. And to all questions the Count Palatine has learned to reply, "Ask my majordomo!" Holberg clearly despises the innkeeper and several tradesmen who are defrauded because, in hopes of obtaining great favors, they wantonly hand over goods to the smooth-tongued majordomo. Altogether the classical comedy has a predilection for the crafty swindler who lives at the expense of other people who will not follow common sense.

The Arabian Powder builds on this idea. In Epistle 117 Holberg begins, "Among many things that men take great pains to discover and which can bring no benefit, is alchemy, or the quest for the philosopher's stone." And at the same time he rejoices that it will scarcely be possible for anyone to transmute cheap metals into gold, and if they did it would create great economic confusion. So when two gallows birds get together to persuade a fanatical alchemist that he can learn the art from them, then it is only right and reasonable that the alchemist is tricked out of 4,000 rix-dollars. He is cured of his folly, and the sum is the tuition fee of reason. The fraud has a solid basis. One of the rogues sits on the square selling some gold powder, but only to those who ask for Arabian powder. And in this way the operation succeeds, as long as stocks last, at least in the goldmaker's mind, and he repeats thrice the Arabian magic formula: *Loof a uoy dna sduarf era srekamdlog!* To his disadvantage the goldmaker discovers too late that these words are to be read backwards thus: Goldmakers are frauds and you a fool!

X *Parodies*

Under contract with Salomon von Qvoten, traveling companies from time to time performed German plays in Copenhagen, making inroads into the profits of the Danish theater by their competition. So as to ridicule the long-drawn-out plots and the exaggerated effects of these so-called Haupts- und Staatsaktionen, Holberg wrote a parody comedy in 1724 called *Ulysses von Ithacia, or a German Comedy.* The twenty-year events of the Iliad and the Odyssey are packed into its five acts, and the playwright, inspired by Homeric parodies on the Italian stage, plays tricks with time and place, and even breaks the dramatic illusion. Holberg deals with several days of decisive battles between the Greeks and the Trojans, but not with the ten years the Greeks had besieged Troy. In the Odyssey we follow King Ulysses on the last part of his journey home to Troy, and in a long inserted account we are given Ulysses's tale of the ten years which the perilous journey had taken him. Holberg begins with the origin of the expedition against Troy—the judgment of Paris and the apple of discord. Instead of the Greek kings assailing Troy, Holberg sends other ancient, indeed even biblical, generals to Troy. Ulysses is there too, and after the fall of Troy we follow him on his journey home, where, unlike in the Odyssey, in which he finds his wife Penelope faithfully waiting, she has cuckolded him ridiculously. When Ulysses's men are changed into swine, Chilian, his servant, transforms them back again by giving them a sound thrashing. The swine then get up and say to Chilian (whose part was played in 1724 by Henrik Wegner) "for sooth that we are honest, *you* shall repay us for these blows, Monsieur Wegner; how impudent of you to ruin the whole story in this way." In the brilliant final scene two Jews appear who have hired out the costumes to the theater and they tear the clothes from Ulysses without listening to his claim that he is a mighty general who has just razed the city of Troy to the ground. This play is a perfect example of the use of dramatic irony.

Presumably from the same year is *Melampe*, a "tragicomedy" in five acts. In his *Histories of Heroes* (1739) Holberg says that Sulla's Roman reign of terror and his remarkable abdication are true tragicomedy, in which terror and despair enhance the effect of the happy outcome. *Melampe* depicts a war which is against the order of nature because it is being fought between two sisters. The bloody strife comes to a happy conclusion when their brother kills the object of the quarrel: a lapdog. In France tragicomedy was a dignified drama which, in contrast to tragedy, ended happily. In Holberg's tragicomedy the people of fashion express themselves in polished alexandrines, while peasants and servants communicate in straightforward prose. In Epistle 249 Holberg calls *Melampe* a parody of tragedies. "Its merit is this: laughter-provoking material is presented in sumptuous and poetic verse, so that the spectators can be moved by it to both tears and laughter." We know that a few of Racine's tragedies were translated for the Lille Grønnegade theater, but, as we can see, Holberg's attitude to elevated style was ironical. The alexandrines of his tragicomedy were fashioned with diligence and finesse, but they express only a couple of hysterical females moaning over a lapdog. As the dramatic irony in *Ulysses* marks the wildest farce, burlesque, within Holberg's comic art, so *Melampe* is the upward limit he reaches in the direction of tragic pathos.

XI   The Journey to Paris

Holberg had written the first Danish play that was performed on the new stage, and it fell to him to write a short play,

The Funeral of Danish Comedy, which, with a regular play, was presented at the farewell performance on Febuary 25, 1727. During the whole period 1722–27 Holberg had been living the exciting life of a playwright, and in his prefaces and memoirs he noted how some of his comedies were received. If all was not well he tried to revise them between performances or from the first printed edition to the second. He was also to experience professional jealousy. As early as in the preface to the 1723 edition, his mouthpiece, Just Justesen, explains that several plays, such as Molière's *Tartuffe* or his doctor comedies are not at all suitable for our theater, for we have not got the sort of confessors envisaged in *Tartuffe* and Danish physicians are so splendid anyway. Holberg liked to see his own comedies on the placards every day. And he also wished to see them performed outside Denmark.

In the summer of 1725 Holberg took leave of absence from the university to make a journey to Aachen for the sake of his health. He was, he explains, fatigued after the hectic writing of so many comedies. But in Amsterdam he changed his mind and traveled via Germany and Brussels to Paris. On his way through Germany he asked about the theater in Bremen, but was told that only traveling troupes gave performances from time to time. In Flanders and Brabant, as he relates in Epistle 48, he was pleased because "I have been able to spend every night in a town of considerable size and of an evening go to the opera or the theater directly upon arrival by carriage." And in Paris not only did he go evening after evening to the Théâtre Français and the Théâtre Italien, but he tried to interest the leader of the Italian company, Riccoboni, in his comedies. "To pass the time," he translated two of his comedies into French. He had brought them with him in his suitcase! He sent a résumé of *The Political Tinker* to Riccoboni, who was spending the summer at the court at Fontainebleau. At first this man of the theater seems to have appreciated what was sent, but he later revised his view, and this was a great disappointment to Holberg.

It is probable that the secret goal of this journey never had been the warm springs of Aachen, but the theaters of Paris, which he hoped to lay at his feet. Mostly, probably, for the sake of the honor and glory, but perhaps also in hope of profits.

In any case, in 1728 Holberg says that "I am now liberated from all the alarm, envy, and labor that constantly weighed me down as long as the comedies lasted. That is all the fruit my work has brought me, but in France or England the author of a successfully produced comedy can often make two or three thousand rix-dollars." But he was not short of money on this journey. Whereas before 1716 he saved as much as possible on transport and lodging, this time he traveled in comfort, and although prices were high in Paris at that time, he does not complain. He was no longer traveling as a nameless student with a travel stipend, but as a professor conscious of his rank. In Paris, in Amsterdam, and in Hamburg, he visited men of learning and singularity. For instance in Paris he visited the famous Jesuit father Hardouin, who loved to put forward paradoxical propositions, e.g., that the sources of ancient history were made up in the Middle Ages. It was on this subject that he entertained Holberg. Another Jesuit, Father Castel, told his guest about an instrument which he had designed in which colors took the place of tones.

Presumably in March, 1726, Holberg returned to Copenhagen after about nine months' absence. Before the theater closed, he managed to write a few comedies, among them *The Invisible Lovers*, which bears traces of fresh theatrical impressions. At the Théâtre Italien Holberg had seen harlequinades by the young dramatist Marivaux, and two of them were of importance for Holberg's new play: *Arlequin poli par l'amour* and *Le prince travesti*, but otherwise Holberg took time to conclude the longer poetic work which he had begun before his journey: *Metamorphosis* (1726). It is an odd attempt at a serious epic. Just as Ovid had made a garland of epic tales into a cycle of poems he entitled *Metamorphoses*, so Holberg describes here, alternately in alexandrines and in short lines, how various animals fall in a war between the two divinities Sylvanus and Flora. Each section in Ovid ends with the transformation of a human being into an animal or plant, and in Holberg the dead animals and plants become human beings in whom their characters live on. The oak becomes the patriarch of stiff people like statesmen and generals; the jackdaw becomes a barber; the fox, an ambassador, and so on. But woven into the satire are elegiac sections approaching the pastoral. In the preface to this long and strange poem, which still awaits proper evaluation within the history of European poetry, Hans Mickelsen bids farewell to writing: "This will without doubt be my last poetical work. Merry poets (sans comparaison) are like cats who decline from a superfluity of playfulness imparted to them by nature into overmuch seriousness."

CHAPTER 6

The Autobiography of a Man in His Prime

AT this time Holberg clearly begins to sense that a period of his life is drawing to a close. He takes stock in himself; he begins to write his memoirs. On December 31, 1727, when he had just reached the age of forty-three, he concluded his first Latin *Letter to a Man of Renown* (*Epistola ad virum perillustrem*). This unnamed character is doubtless fictitious. This was the first part of Holberg's autobiography and was published in 1728. It is altogether a wonderfully vivid piece of writing, entirely devoted to the experiences, writings, and character of its author.

Altogether the work, known as *Memoirs,* consists of four parts, three autobiographical letters written in Latin, which appeared in 1728, 1737, and 1743; then at his death in 1754 Holberg left a letter in Danish (numbered as Epistle 447) which was intended as a continuation of the history of his life. These four letters together form a consecutive account of Holberg's life.

It is in the nature of things that each of these letters has its own particular character determined by its content. The first letter is dominated by his journeys abroad. Each journey has its own particular purpose, but together they form the journey through Europe of a student, Holberg's *peregrinatio academica.* The second autobiographical letter preserves firsthand impressions of the great fire which ravaged Copenhagen in October, 1728. The third letter has only a few personal experiences to relate. By this time Holberg was approaching sixty, and reflection is supplanting narration. Complete books are inserted into this letter, evaluations of some of the nations of Europe are given, there is an attempt at a system of morality, and there are six Latin essays which, a year later, in Danish translation, were to be included in *Moral Thoughts.* The fourth letter (Epistle

447) is the work of an old man. The facts are presented almost at random; new themes are introduced with little attempt to link them with what precedes them. In justice it should perhaps be mentioned that Holberg did not supervise the publication of this letter.

Memoirs is the usual contemporary word applied to works resembling Holberg's and it was in fact the title given to the English translation, *Memoirs of Lewis Holberg* (1827). The book deals with the personality of its author, but there is also another important theme: his works. There is a curious difference in the way Holberg treats his character and his works. He does not laud his conduct or set his experiences in a favorable light. He gives a lowly picture of himself as an impecunious and sick man dragging himself along the roads of Europe. But when his works are concerned, he brooks no compromise. He will not tolerate one derogatory word; there must not be the slightest stain upon his honor as an author. In these autobiographical letters, then, Holberg makes no great claims for himself, only for his books.

Among the models Holberg took for his autobiographical letters, he mentions Pliny the Younger. Here he is thinking mainly of his Latin style, which bears many resemblances to Pliny's *Epistles*, although Holberg does not attempt to imitate Pliny's polish. There is greater resemblance in content, however, to be seen in the directness with which both Pliny and Holberg recount the events both small and great of their personal experience. But Pliny's epistles are essays, small compositions about a wide variety of subjects. Holberg's letters were chronologically composed. The scheme of them was the academic *vita*, as it was found in the Latin *programmata* of the University, recounting the lifework of deceased professors and others and containing information about the subject's family, education, career, and literary activity. In these and similar biographies which made up a special division in the printed funeral orations, detailed information about the travels of the subject played an important part. In addition it is probable that Holberg was influenced by some of the many contemporary books of travel memoirs, but it is impossible to determine which these were. He may have been acquainted with other kinds of memoirs. That at first and second hand he was acquainted with various French memoirists we know, for instance, from his *Moral Thoughts* and his *Histories of Heroines*.

If we look at the first autobiographical letter, the first part of the *Memoirs*, we can easily discover the two motives that moved Holberg to write. One was the urge to give an account of himself, to describe events with his own person in the center. And the other motive was his desire to make known to the reading public of Europe that Denmark now had a modern literature, and that he, Ludvig Holberg, had written it. In the very earliest of the letters he reviews the contents of his first fifteen comedies, presumably in order to attract foreign translators. In the third autobiographical letter he writes of his own *Church History*: "Those who would translate this into other languages would not find their labor unrewarded." He wrote this in 1743. *Church History* had appeared in 1738 and he was impatient, but he had to wait until 1749 before it came out in German translation. With his *Histories of Heroes* (written in 1739) the case was different, for a German translation had appeared in 1741; therefore he writes in the same letter: "I do not need to give a detailed description of this work, since it has been translated into German and is known to those abroad." There seems to be no connection between the urge to confess and the desire for fame abroad. Holberg does not share with a number of other "confessors" the desire to find fame through self-revelation.

Holberg achieved what he had set out to achieve. His *Memoirs* have caused both his contemporaries and later generations to talk about him. Shortly after the publication of the first letter, his colleague, Professor Hans Gram, wrote a letter in Latin to his friend Professor Fabricius in Hamburg. In this he has occasion to mention Holberg's works, including the recently published autobiographical letter. He remarks that the anecdotes recorded by the author and his praise of his own writings might give his enemies, if he had any, occasion to laugh at him.

It is in large measure due to his Latin autobiography that Holberg was the first Dane to be given a place in a work of reference, *Geschichte jetzlebender Gelehrten*, which a clergyman in Hanover, E. L. Rathler, published in twelve volumes 1740–46.

As is natural, the editor of this work tends to pick out passages in which Holberg discusses his studies abroad and his conversations with well-known scholars. Some fifty years later another German discovered Holberg's *Memoirs*. He was Johann Georg Müller; he was not primarily attracted to Holberg as a scholar but by the frankness of his narrative. Rousseau's *Confessions* had appeared in 1781–88 and, with a view to gathering an anthology of self-revelatory works, Müller founded a series of works with the title *Bekenntnisse merkwürdiger Männer von sich selbst*, 1791–1810; vol. 2, 1793, contains excerpts from Holberg's autobiography.

All three autobiographical letters had appeared in German by 1745 and in Dutch in 1766. They were translated into English in 1827, but as early as February, 1755, Oliver Goldsmith had heard of Holberg's travels in Europe without money. Goldsmith, who was at that time studying medicine at Leyden, was encouraged by Holberg's example and journeyed through France and Italy, begging and singing his way as he believed that Holberg had done before him. Some years later, in 1759, he published *An Enquiry into the Present State of Polite Learning in Europe*. In three brief pages Goldsmith presents Holberg's career as a model of his own. This is a delightfully confused echo of Holberg's memoirs.

Holberg's autobiography had, of course, most significance for his dual fatherland. The first two letters were translated from Latin by a Norwegian theologian Thomas Georg Krogh in 1741. In 1745 a translation of all three letters appeared. With his autobiography Holberg has given color and vividness to all later presentations of his life. What would our works on Holberg be like without the vivid wealth of personal experience and the interpretations given to us in these autobiographical letters? We can answer this question by referring to Molière. There are many documents relating to Molière's life, but we completely lack the plenitude of openings for fruitful research to be found in Holberg's autobiographical writings. And so we must be grateful to Holberg's literary exhibitionism, which saved his biography from being merely an account of his works.

To illustrate this and to demonstrate the general character of Holberg's writings, we give an extended quotation from the

second letter, in which Holberg speaks of his own character.
This quotation is presented in the anonymous English translation
of 1827 as it has been edited by S. E. Fraser (1970).

I should now bring this narrative to a conclusion, if it did not seem
necessary to add something by way of finish, touching my character
and manners; for as few persons of the order of professors have been
more exposed to the criticism of their fellow-citizens, I may perhaps
be allowed in my turn to draw my own portrait with the same pencil
which has sketched the portraits of so many other men.

I was sensible from my earliest years, that nothing was so injurious
to my health as indulgence in what are commonly termed pleasures.
Accordingly I lived so sparingly and frugally, that though a boy in
years, I seemed to my youthful companions an old man in habits. My
extreme temperance and severity of manners often exposed me to
raillery and facetiousness, which, as I was extremely choleric, I did
not very patiently digest. Nevertheless, I made no alteration in my
mode of living, but rather increased the severity of my regimen with
my increasing years. Thus I was in the habit, when a boy, of drinking
wine greatly diluted with water; but in manhood I abjured wine altogether, deeming it poison to my constitution. At length, not satisfied
with my accustomed habits of frugality, I endeavored to limit myself
to certain measured portions of meat and drink, imitating the example
of certain persons who have declared this mathematical sort of diet
to be wonderfully salutary. My friends attributed this resolution not
to philosophy, but to absolute folly; they often expostulated with me
upon what they considered a deplorable infatuation, and contended
that I was to all practical purposes a dead man; for to eat apart from
the rest of the world, said they, is to live out of the pale of society;
and what can be more absurd than to withdraw yourself from the
society of mankind in the flower of your age? I replied, that sociality
did not consist in eating and drinking; but this argument made not
the slightest impression. Others, whose reasoning powers were of a
denser description, assassinated me with commonplaces and texts of
scripture which they did not understand, declaring that to weigh
what you ate and drank, was nothing short of distrusting the providence of God, and that there were instances of persons who by thus
protracting life had incurred the divine wrath. To this I replied, that
I did not recollect any instances in which the divine wrath had been
manifested on that account; and that if any such instances were to be
met with in books, I should put the same faith in them as in a nursery
tale. I remembered indeed that this charge was made against John
Chrysostom in a certain synod; but the accusation was of a piece with

many other ridiculous charges made against him in the same synod. I added, that it behoved every man to endeavor by all possible care and attention to secure and preserve that first of blessings, a sound mind in a sound body. But these arguments availed nothing against the unceasing expostulations of my friends; and I found that the only chance I had of escaping from their importunities, was to say nothing in my defense.

The complaint under which I labor, I inherit from my father; for diseases as well as other possessions are acquired by succession. I take no medicine, because I am ignorant of the source of my disorder. Sometimes a torpor comes over my whole body, and at these periods I may be seen walking like a snail; at other times I walk with surprising velocity; sometimes I am seized with pains in my head, at other times the enemy attacks my feet. The stomach is often the seat of my disorder, and then I feel alternate heat and cold in that quarter; sometimes there is too much fermentation, and sometimes none whatever in it. For two years I was afflicted with a severe headache which compelled me to abstain from all meditation. During this time I read nothing but the journals and historical works; but my disease having shifted to another quarter, at the end of two years I took great pleasure in philosophical speculations, and in poetry. I then wrote my heroic poem, with the satires and comedies of which I have given an account in this narrative. Hence I manage my complaints according to my own judgment, without taking advice about them; for I believe physicians would waste their time in attempting to subdue a malady which assumes a variety of shapes. My mind is differently affected, according to the state of my bodily health; and it is my great object to prevent these mental affections from running into excess. The affections I allude to, are joy, sorrow, fear, courage, torpor, alacrity, enthusiasm, indifference; and these prevail according to the excess of vicious humors in different parts of my body. Thus when my disease attacked the region of the heart, I used formerly to be seized with a mania for reform, and inveighed vehemently against the depravity of mankind. As soon as the complaint shifted to another part of the body, no one could be more indulgent to human frailities than myself. Hence, whenever I feel this desire of reforming mankind coming upon me, experience has taught me that I should attack, not mankind, but my own bowels; for my enthusiasm invariably gives way to a few laxative pills; and as soon as these have operated the world appears to me with quite a different aspect.

I am apt to be too fastidious in my estimate of social qualities, as some men are too delicate in the choice of their food; for there is scarcely one man in a hundred whose society I can endure. One annoys me with his conversation, another with his gestures; in short, I have been compelled to retire with disgust from most of my acquaintances, and to seek consolation in solitude. As there is nothing I admire more than brevity, so there is no class of men I abominate more than those inveterate prosers who assassinate their victims with long dissertations and interminable narratives. I have suffered so much from persons of this description, that I have often thought the same fate awaited me which Sabella predicts for Horace:

> He shall not perish by poison or sword,
> Nor lumbago nor gout this man shall lay low,
> His death blow shall come by a chatterbox' tongue.

Of all the comedies I have written, *Gert Westphaler, The Babbling Barber* pleases me most, because it exposes that pertinacious garrulity from which I have suffered so much torture. I have been censured for avoiding people of this description, by those who do not distinguish hostility from disgust; for you may be very much disgusted with an individual, aginst whom you entertain no sort of hostility.

There are some who consider my satires too severe; and I confess that many of them are written with much bitterness; but I attack vices, not individuals. I am aware, indeed, that this kind of writing is generally disliked, and that the office of the satirist is a most invidious one. We see flatterers loaded with honors, while men who have the honesty and the courage to blame where censure is called for, are denounced as bad citizens. Honest satirists are hated, because their medicine is disagreeable, though salutary; fawning sycophants are applauded, because the potions they administer are pleasant, though they confirm and exasperate the disease. The former are the true friends, while they are deemed the enemies of mankind; the latter, while they appear to be the friends, are in reality the deadliest foes of the human race.

CHAPTER 7

From Dramatist to Historian

I Description of Denmark and Norway

IN 1727 activity was suspended for several years at the Copenhagen theater. By that time Holberg had begun to turn his
attention to the study of history. After his poetic frenzy there
followed a historical frenzy to vie with it. An artist by temperament, he became like one possessed. In the course of some dozen
years he published a long series of historical works.

For some time he had been nursing the idea of a vast *Description of Denmark and Norway* along the same lines as the English
work *The Present State of Great Britain* by Edward Chamberlayne, which had first appeared in 1668–71 and had been reprinted many times. Holberg had used it when he was writing
about England and had admired the sound judgment behind
Chamberlayne's arrangement of the chapters and the presentation, enlivened with quotations and anecdotes. In 1729 Holberg
was able to carry out his plan of writing a similar work about
Denmark-Norway, and the result demonstrates the mastery of
composition that was now his. He was not content to describe
the present state of the two kingdoms; in almost every chapter
he returns to the origins. Among other things he gives information
about national character past and present as well as the history
of government, of religious and academic institutions, of the
social classes, of trade, and of the fiscal and judicial systems. On
most of these subjects there already existed a whole scholarly
literature that was tedious to read and formless. Holberg drew
from this literature what he needed in order to produce a well-
documented, well-balanced, and well-written book. This *Description of Denmark and Norway* makes us think of the *Siècle de
Louis XIV*, which Voltaire presumably commenced about 1732
and of which he published two chapters in 1739—about ten years

89

after Holberg's work. It was, however, not until 1751 that the first complete edition of *Siècle de Louis XIV* appeared. Like Voltaire, Holberg remained a creative writer even when dealing with historical subjects, and, also like Voltaire, he replaced a historical chronicle of facts about wars with a history of manners and customs.

The plan of the book was based on Chamberlayne's work. In the opening chapter, "On the Nature and Qualities of the Danish Nation," he first spends some time on the bravery of the old Norsemen and their contempt for death. Without pointing out the connection between past and present, he finds among "my countrymen" (i.e., the Norwegians) a valor without parallel in modern times. In this serious work Holberg even finds room to express his personal attitude: "Among all the peoples I know, I am incommoded least by the company of Danes. A Frenchman slays me with grimaces, a German with pretentious chatter, an Englishman irritates me with his self-adulation, a Spaniard with his dignified mien." The following excerpts from this chapter of the book will give an idea of his penetrating comments:

Nowadays the Danes are regarded as a well-mannered and highly civilized people, particularly the inhabitants of Copenhagen, who apply great diligence to the education of their children, holding to both civility and learning. For it is not unusual here to see little children, and even those of the middle classes, who are trained in many skills and can speak two or three foreign languages with great proficiency, so that foreigners visiting the country are obliged to admit that they have seen nothing like this elsewhere. They are particularly amazed at the young ladies who, though never having been abroad, can speak to foreigners in their own tongue and commend themselves as much thereby as by their natural beauty. Young men often travel abroad to perfect the languages learned in childhood and to observe the manners and customs of other nations. In this nation is found a remarkable modesty, for whereas most other nations have a high opinion of themselves and look down on others, the Danes usually speak highly of others, which, although nowadays often looked upon as a vice, must be accounted one of the rarest and greatest virtues.

Holberg has, however, a number of faults to find with the Danes. In the following passage he enumerates five:

I find it not without reason that a certain indolence is ascribed to them. So that people of fashion die of scurvy because they will not exert themselves to walk from one house to another, and common people die of poverty because they have little affection for work. One observes that a thirst for honor obtains among them, each wants to be given a better seat than the others at gatherings. Then they admire anything that comes from foreign parts, from which arises the misfortune that all, however small their abilities, travel abroad and return naked. They are too ready to adopt foreign fashions and have too great a taste for foreign wares, one of the results being that the handicrafts of the country often make little progress. There is a desire to know something about everything, which means that even the best brains seldom reach perfection in one field. It is common here to meet people who speak four or five languages. Other nations, particularly the French, English, and Italians, limit their studies, know but one language but that thoroughly, understand but one science, but to perfection. In England I have observed among musicians that few can handle more than one instrument, so that each reaches perfection in his own instrument. Finally, this people can with justice be reproached for becoming slaves of certain unnecessary fashions, which are particularly burdensome economically, so that this country, and especially Copenhagen, has become one of the most expensive places in Europe in which to live.

In his chapter on Danish goverent Holberg rebuts with examples from history the attack of the English historian Robert Molesworth on Danish absolutism. Freedom and independence, he maintains, would be of great utility for human beings, if they were not subject to passions. In his chapter on religion, Holberg begins with the religion of the Vikings and continues with a brief outline of Danish church history. Altogether the book is full of useful information, which even nowadays can be read with profit as giving an understanding of the outlook of absolutism's golden age.

II   History of the Kingdom of Denmark

The completion of the *Description of Denmark and Norway* left Holberg free to plunge into serious historical writing. He set himself the very highest goals when writing history, and the pace and energy with which he set to work are quite remarkable. His *History of the Kingdom of Denmark*, which appeared in three volumes in 1732, 1733, and 1735, runs to about 2,500 pages. In his preface to the first volume Holberg mentions his frailty and his exhausted body and cites "a pagan of antiquity" for saying that "whom Jupiter hates he makes an author." He asserts that he only continues because it is a task that must be performed.

Holberg's long history of Denmark is divided into five periods. The first is the ancient heathen period. He rejects the fabulous register of kings traditionally accepted and begins with King Skjold. His second division spans the period from the introduction of Christianity to the uniting of the three Scandinavian kingdoms under Queen Margaret (the Kalmar Union of 1397). The third period stretches from the Kalmar Union to Christian II (reigned 1513–23). This division into periods seems to suggest that the concept of the Middle Ages, with which Holberg was quite familiar, did not seem to him relevant as a division of the history of Denmark. In the fourth period he traces with disgust the inroads of the aristocracy into royal power until, with the fifth period beginning with the accession of Frederik III (1648), he can celebrate the arrival of absolutism. This fifth period concludes the book with the death of Frederik III in 1670. Each period is introduced with political and cultural surveys, a kind of stock-taking. Within the periods the reigns of the various kings form a fixed framework and each king's death gives opportunity for a detailed summing-up of the achievements of his reign and an evaluation of his character. On this important point Holberg is more thorough than his model, a large history of England, *Histoire de l'Angleterre*, which began to appear in 1724. The author of this was Paul de Rapin de Thoyras, a French lawyer and army officer who had fled to England in 1686 because of his reformed faith. He was no great intellect, but was an honest seeker after truth and wrote with facility. His work of many volumes was quickly sold out and was reprinted and even trans-lated into English. In this work Holberg had seen a modern national history and was inspired to imitation. He was also moved to limit his material: in ten heavy volumes Rapin de Thoyras got as far as 1688 and after his death other hands added three more volumes to bring the history up to 1727.

Politically, Holberg's work is a royalist citizen's account of the history of Denmark. Philosophically, it is a humanist's evaluation of events and persons. In sundry passages an "unbiased consideration" of history is developed. In the third volume, partly on the basis of unprinted sources, Holberg introduces a detailed biography of Griffenfeld. Griffenfeld (1635–99), originally Peder Schumacher, was the son of a German wine merchant who had settled in Copenhagen. Extremely precocious, he was of service to the new absolute monarchy seeking advisers outside the ranks of the nobility and soon reached a pinnacle of power. His enemies took advantage of his handling of foreign affairs, in which he compromised himself, and he was sentenced to death (1676), to be reprieved on the scaffold. The rest of his life he spent in confinement. Holberg concludes his account of his life with a comparative characterization of three Danish statesmen who had all known what it was to rise high and fall low: Corfitz Ulfeldt (1609–64), a gifted nobleman and son-in-law of Christian IV who was long exiled for high treason; Hannibal Sehested (1609–66), a once powerful figure who fell from favor; and Griffenfeld.

From a literary-historical point of view Holberg's *History of the Kingdom of Denmark* is a stylistic achievement. Previous Danish historians were Anders Sørensen Vedel, who in 1575 had translated the Latin of Saxo Grammaticus into down-to-earth Danish. In 1595 Arild Huitfeldt had compiled a Danish chronicle in involved language (see Chapter 2). Now suddenly, with no transition, Holberg writes his history in a historian's dignified prose. In his comedies we are often given glimpses of Copenhagen colloquialism and dialect. When writing history, Holberg aims at a literary and balanced language. The gayness of the comedies appears only at very long intervals; for instance, when Holberg has related that in the Battle of Fodevig (1134) five bishops and sixty clergymen fell, he allows himself to comment: "Poor students had cause to rejoice at the great battle, because so many livings fell vacant on the same day." Apart from these rare gleams of humor, the Muse of History is a solemn lady for Holberg and history a serious genre. In his *History of the Kingdom of Denmark* he establishes a linguistic norm with a fairly fixed pattern of main and subordinate clauses carrying his description and evaluation along in a calm and measured rhythm.

As a writer Holberg never loses the broad view; he has, never-theless, an artistic sense of detail which recreates the situation before the eyes of the reader. As a short sample of Holberg's ability, we may quote his brief, lucid, objective, yet warm de-scription of Copenhagen under siege. During a war with Sweden Copenhagen was invested by the Swedes in 1658. In the autumn of that year the Swedes tightened their grip on the city and Hol-berg's account of the situation is this:

And now a great scarcity began in Copenhagen, for all supplies were stopped both by land and by sea. The Swedes could not have commenced the siege at a more favorable time for themselves and a more difficult time for the city, for, as is known, not only Copen-hagen but the people of the whole kingdom lay in their food supplies at harvest time and, as winter sets in, they store up what they will need for the whole year. The cellars and larders were practically empty at the beginning of the siege; the corn was still standing in the fields and much of the grass had not yet been mown. As the city was filled with an unusually large number of people, it was easy to calcu-late that there would soon be a lack of food. And this calculation did not prove incorrect, for as soon as winter commenced, a rise in the price of all goods was noticeable. In this situation His Majesty made it a special concern that traders did not take overdue advantage but charged reasonable prices for their wares, and likewise that households limited their housekeeping, so that a meal for people of standing was a spoonful of soup, some salted meat or buttered bread, and the in-habitants as it were vied with one another in frugality. In this His Majesty also set them a good example, being content with the same diet as the common man and refusing completely to live in other manner than to share with the soldiers their hardships and labor.

III   *The Professor of History*

In 1730 Holberg became professor of history and geography in the University of Copenhagen. The governing body of the university (consistorium) set him the task of compiling textbooks in these two disciplines; in 1732 both disciplines were made subjects in the philosophical examination, which was compulsory for all students at the university. It is uncertain how much profit the students gained from Professor Holberg's lectures, but the two surveys he wrote in Latin as textbooks, on world history *Synopsis historiæ universalis,* and on geography *Compendium geograph-icum,* both published in 1733, were reprinted several times and translated and revised. Holberg shows that he has ability as a teacher: the subject is arranged in clear divisions, the style is terse and pithy. In order to assist the memories of his readers, he incorporated short and vivid characterizations into the closely packed array of facts. For example, under the history of Russia he mentions the city of Novgorod and quotes the proverb: "Who dare assail God or the great Novgorod?"

From June, 1735, to May, 1736, Holberg was rector of the University. At the traditional ceremony in the consistorium building (still existing) at which he handed on the office to his successor, Marcus Wøldike, professor of theology, he delivered a Latin oration in which, in dignified phrases, he put forward a philosopher's views on the granting of stipends, the promotion of study, and the difficulties a rector encounters when certain powerful personalities frustrate his efforts by their party spirit. As a philosopher he must remain firm as long as there is hope of a solution, but when the matter has been concluded, then he may calmly accept things as they are and admit defeat, even though he is not convinced. Otherwise his strength will be regarded as willfulness, and his firmness will be called obstinacy. In 1737 he became the university's "quaestor" or bursar, and he proved to have a good grasp of accounts. He was given leave from his lecturing duties for this task. The sound business sense he had shown in his own affairs now benefited the university.

IV General Church History

In 1737 Holberg published a volume of Latin *Opuscula latina.* This included a reprint of his first autobiographical epistle, to which he appended a brief *Epistola secunda.* In this he describes the great fire of Copenhagen of 1728, which reduced about two-fifths of the city, including Holberg's own house, to ashes. His description is full of vivid details modeled on Pliny the Younger's account of the eruption of Vesuvius in A.D. 79 and of a city fire in Asia Minor. In this contemporary reporting Holberg is more of a rhetorician than a historian, and indeed most of this description is taken over almost word for word from his memorial oration on Frederik IV in 1730.

In this second autobiographical letter the author mentions his completed *History of the Kingdom of Denmark*, which he calls a desperate work (opus desperatum). In the preface to a collection of Latin epigrams which are printed in the same volume, he confides to the reader that he is now working on a *General Church History*, and this appeared in 1738. It begins with a masterly résumé of the gospels, the history of Jesus Christ, and concludes with the life and work of Luther. In sixteen chapters, each dealing with a century, a curve is drawn which reminds one of the pattern in his *History of the Kingdom of Denmark*: first the Early Church with its authentic and wholesome Christianity, which is then perverted under the secularization of the papal power, to break forth again at the Reformation. Throughout, the style reflects Holberg's attitude to his subject: "I have cut my pen according to my matter," he says in the preface. Therefore the serious tone he employs when describing the first centuries gives way to a rallying style in the later centuries. It is the scholarly virtue of this church history that it juxtaposes the ecclesiastical and the profane. The author knows that religious disputes gave rise to violent changes in state organization and that statesmen often used religion as a pretext for political intervention. Holberg's critical view of the external policy of the Pope sharpened his insight into the connection between ecclesiastical and profane history.

For this reason it is remarkable that in Holberg's *Jewish History*, which appeared in 1742 in two weighty volumes, he sees the marvelous history of the Jews as "written by the finger of God," as a mirror of "God's wondrous economy, of his love, long-suffering, omnipotence, wisdom, and infinitely strict justice." It is only as the fulfillment of a divine command that one can understand how the Jews, though scattered over the whole world, paradoxically preserved their language, laws, customs, religion, and ceremonies. For Holberg, history is the history of man; he does not see the footprint of God in history as Bossuet had done in the previous century and as Grundtvig was to do in the next. But the miraculous history of the Jews was for Holberg the rationalist the exception that proved the rule.

Between his *Church History* and his *Jewish History* Holberg attempted biography. Plutarch had placed biographies of Greeks and Romans in pairs, giving an account of, for instance, two orators, Demosthenes and Cicero, and then comparing them. In his *Comparative Histories of Heroes* (1739) Holberg introduces each pair of biographies with an essay dealing with the qualities of his subjects, and he concludes with a comparison. For the sake of novelty he selects several Asiatic rulers and people from ancient Mexico and Peru. Most interesting are his views on Sulla, whom he sets alongside Caesar, and on Socrates, whom he compares with Epaminondas. The book was a success, and Holberg followed it up with *Comparative Histories of Heroines* (1745), which was similarly arranged. In this, however, he developed a philosophical or psychological idea in each introductory essay and the biographies were adduced as examples. Thus the histories of the Danish Queen Margaret and the English Queen Elizabeth go to show that the abilities and character of a sovereign are of greater significance for a country than is the form of government. The lives of Cleopatra and Anne Boleyn show that some women captivate men by yielding, others by aloofness.

As a historian Holberg is always steeped in his material. He is interested in subjects for which there are abundant sources to draw upon. This means that he will not deal with periods that are obscurely documented. He will admit ancient history, though not at just any price. He despises speculation and rejects archeology as groveling in dunghills—his curiosity has its limits! If there are no respectable written sources, then there is no history; where those are lacking the historian has no business.

CHAPTER 8

The Struggle for Tolerance

I Niels Klim

IN his Latin oration in memory of King Frederik IV, Holberg praised the reign of this king as an age when "words had free play in the land; we acted comedies and fearlessly outdid one another in jest." During the reign of Christian VI (1730–1746), however, the situation changed. The new king and queen were wholehearted supporters of the Pietist movement, which had originated in Germany in the previous century. Reacting against rigid, external orthodoxy, the German theologians Spener and Francke had called for a Christianity that was more vital and practical. Only those who through crisis and conversion had reached the security of faith could reckon themselves as saved. With Christian zeal the saved could bring pressure to bear on the unsaved. Under Christian VI Pietist clergy gained great influence through new regulations concerning church festivals (1735), through the introduction of confirmation in 1736, and by the establishment of the College of General Church Inspection in 1737. By the prohibition of nonconformist sects in the Conventicle Act of 1741, the authority of parish clergy was strengthened against sectarian movements. Pietism, originally a struggle against official Christianity, had become the state religion.

In humanistic circles there was little enthusiasm for this new ecclesiastical policy. Holberg had been the victim of this trend in 1731, when an attempt to reestablish the theater in Copenhagen was completely abortive. And in the same year Holberg had published the comedies in five volumes. In 1735, in the final volume of his history of Denmark, Holberg cited Frederik III's banning of conventicles in 1655, but he omitted to add his own "philosophical findings" on this subject. This was an obvi-

98

ously too topical subject and his comments were not printed until after his death. Holberg's first reply to state Pietism was the Latin romance *Nicolai Klimii iter subterraneum* (Niels Klim's Underground Journey) of 1741. Official pressure upon thought in Denmark had opened Holberg's eyes to the intolerance against which the most enlightened men in Europe were fighting, men such as Locke in England, Leibniz and Thomasius in Germany, and Voltaire and Montesquieu in France.

Montesquieu and Swift had each shown how one's own society could be satirized. In the former's *Lettres Persanes* (1721) foreigners, in this case two Persians, come to Paris and view life there with sharp and critical eyes. In *Gulliver's Travels* (1726, Danish translation 1768), on the other hand, an Englishman himself travels abroad to exotic regions and meets fantastic caricatures of the way of life from which he has come. Holberg chose the second method for satirizing his own society and, like many of his predecessors, he chose to write in Latin, but this was not in order to conceal bold opinions behind a learned language, but to secure his book a wide dissemination.

Nicolai Klimii iter subterraneum, which appeared in Leipzig anonymously, gained access everywhere in Europe and was translated into many languages. As Swift does, Holberg makes the widely traveled man the narrator of his own experiences. This form is derived from travelogues. But Holberg sets the journey in the interior of the earth. A man with a theological degree, Niels Klim, is driven by curiosity to enter a natural cave outside Bergen. He tumbles down a shaft and finds himself in the interior of the earth, where he encounters a new world: a subterranean planetary system populated by remarkable beings. Niels travels over the kingdoms of this interior world, describes them and thereby—and this is the point of the romance—has described the kingdoms of the outer earth. In the interior of the globe there are the same follies and virtues as there are outside, but to a more concentrated degree. Each country has its own specialty, and thereby exemplifies a philosophical principle. Holberg employs indirect moralizing—satirical presentation à la Swift—and direct moralizing with the depiction of what is exemplary.

The first country to which Klim comes is Potu, the ideal state.

The name is possibly Utopia reversed. He is expelled from this country when he presents an unfortunate project for excluding women from official positions. He proceeds from the planet Nazar to the subterranean firmament; both on Nazar and on the firmament he visits a number of countries. He achieves success in his new surroundings by exploiting his terrestrial accomplishments. In Martinia, which is mainly modeled upon France, he is honored for introducing the periwig. And in the primitive country of Qvama he becomes emperor because, like Peter the Great, he organizes the kingdom and particularly its war potential. He has cannons made, and he can therefore subdue country after country, but when his authority becomes oppressive, the people rebel, Klim has to flee and conceals himself in a cave. He tumbles into a shaft and ends up outside Bergen, where he had begun. He lives and dies there as a sacristan in that city.

Niels Klim is a romance full of serious and gay paradoxes, a firework display of ideas. As a sample of the satire to be found in *Niels Klim* we may cite the passage which describes Klim's experiences in the country of Mardak, where the inhabitants, though similar to one another in body, have eyes of different shapes:

The most numerous and the most powerful race among these tribes is that of the Nagiri, or those who have oval eyes and to whom, consequently, all things appear under an oval form. The Regents, Senators and Priests, are always elected of this tribe. These only manage the affairs of state, and admit no person of the other classes to fill any public appointment, unless he acknowledge that a certain tablet, which is placed in the highest part of the Temple erected in honour of the Sun, appears to him also of an oval shape, and attest the same on oath. This tablet is the most sacred in the Mardakite religion. Many upright and virtuous burghers, who have a great aversion to perjury, never, for that reason, obtain any honourable post, and are continually exposed to all possible ignominy, reproach, and persecution. It avails nothing their excusing, and endeavouring to justify themselves by defending the belief they ought to have in their own eyes: on the contrary they only thereby involve themselves in actions at law, and that which is a natural defect is laid to their charge as mischief and contumacy. The oath to which those who are desirous of being preferred to any office must subscribe is of the following tenor: "I swear that the sacred tablet, placed in the Temple of the Sun, appears to me of an oval shape, and I promise to maintain this opinion until the last moment of my existence." As soon as a person has taken this oath, he is received in the tribe of the Nagiri, and is eligible for any post of honour that he may choose to sue for. . . .

I repaired to the Temple of the Sun, in order to ascertain whether my own eyes were orthodox or not; and as the sacred tablet really appeared to me to be square, I told my landlord, who had lately been appointed churchwarden in the town, candidly what I thought. He heaved a deep sigh on this occasion, and acknowledged in like manner that it appeared to him also square, but that he durst not express his opinion to that effect before any person whomsoever, for fear of quarrelling with the ruling tribe, and losing his appointment.

In silence, but not without a palpitation of the heart and a violent trembling in every limb, I quitted this place, for fear my back should be compelled to atone for the error of my eyes, and that under the odious epithet of heretic, I should be made a laughing-stock of, and disgracefully and ignominiously driven from the town. No regulation or order in the world, as it appeared to me, could be more cruel, barbarous, and unreasonable than this, whereby dissimulation and perjury, of which I was an eye-witness, alone paved the way to posts of honour. I therefore on my return to Potu, did not forget on every occasion, to pour forth my spleen against this barbarous state. But as I was once, according to my custom, fulminating against this regulation and giving vent to the whole of my spite in a dialogue with a most intimate friend, I received the following hint: "We Potuites see clearly enough that the regulations of the Nagiri are absurd and unreasonable, but you, my dear Klim, ought not, as it seemeth to me, to be so much astonished that the inequality of vision should be treated there with so much rigour, for if I remember right, you yourself related that there are, in most European states, certain ruling stocks or tribes, who because of a peculiar defect in their visual organs or understanding persecute the others with fire and sword, and yet you extolled these violent measures as very pious regulations and highly beneficial to the state." I quickly remarked the drift of this rub, and immediately blushed deeply. From that time I always judged those who were apt to err with much less severity and was continually clamorous for toleration. (Quoted from *A Journey to the World Underground*, London, 1828.)

The book, of course, caused trouble, and it was a borderline matter whether it should be confiscated or not. The Copenhagen publisher who had had the book printed in Leipzig to avoid censorship, took advantage of the scandal to raise the price to

one rix-dollar. As we have mentioned, it was quickly translated
into many languages, and it is an interesting thought that in his
own century Holberg achieved the largest number of readers
and disseminated his ideas most widely, not through comedies
or history, but through this fictional travelogue.

II Philosophical Interests

In 1743, when Holberg published his third autobiographical
Epistola, he was very much concerned with the clerical hue and
cry that had been caused by *Niels Klim*. But he also dilated upon
his own philosophical and religious difficulties. He obviously
felt an increasing urge to expound, both to himself and to
others, his religious convictions and for that reason, as a citizen
and a writer, he required freedom to think, to speak, and to
write. As his frenzy for history was ebbing away, a philosophical
frenzy was seizing his soul and this possessed him to the end.
As Holberg was immersing himself in the great philosophical
writers, his literary interests were changing. In the course
of the 1730's Holberg was increasingly taken up with the philosophical writings of Cicero and Seneca. In 1732 he bought at
an auction Seneca's *Opera Omnia* and in Holberg's Latin epigrams of 1737 he set a number of Seneca's apothegms to verse.
He obtained a recent edition (of 1737) of Cicero's *Opera Omnia*
and in his *Histories of Heroes* (1739) it can be seen from the
quotations that Holberg had been studying the examples in,
for instance, Cicero's work *De officiis* (On Duties). In these
Roman philosophers Holberg read about the attitude to life
befitting a wise man. He saw the ancient idea of wisdom presented lucidly and at times cogently.

But the philosophies of the ancients were given a more daring
and up-to-date twist when, in the French Renaissance, they were
taken up by Montaigne, whose *Essais* were first published in
1530–88. Holberg obtained them in an edition of 1739 with some
excellent notes from which he also knew how to profit. Montaigne
made himself the subject of his book. He observed himself and
he did not claim that his findings and conclusions had validity
for others than himself, scarcely indeed even for himself, for he
recognized that man is a changeable, fluid, and chaotic crea-

ture. It is from the title of Montaigne's book that the word
essay has assumed its literary meaning. Montaigne considered
that he was putting his faculties and potentialities for philoso-
phizing to the test (*à l'essai*). As he put forward various surprising propositions, there was right from the beginning of this
new genre a demand for surprising and preferably paradoxical
ideas.

Holberg clearly perceived Montaigne's special quality. In the
chapter *Des livres* Holberg saw brilliant examples of subjective
literary criticism, and in his long third autobiographical *Epistola*
he imitated 'this, going right through his favorite authors and,
like Montaigne, emphasizing that in his verdicts upon them he
was exclusively following his own taste. For instance, when, in
ranking Virgil above Ovid, he comments: "I think I am wrong,
but it has hitherto been impossible for me to refute my error,
because Virgil still seems to me without peer." He prefers Seneca's heavily worked style to Cicero's carefree eloquence. And
Holberg praises Montaigne for his candor: "I should love him
even more highly if he spoke less about himself." An amusing
objection from the self-obsessed author of these epistles. And
finally: "Montaigne's paradoxes appeal to me. By paradoxes I
understand propositions which with good reason conflict with
current opinions."

III   Moral Thoughts

It is with precisely such paradoxes that Holberg concludes
his third autobiographical letter. Here we find Holberg's first
essays: six Latin samples of his philosophy or *systema morale*.
Five of the six articles are constructed upon a lively basic idea:
what is becoming and unbecoming other than what custom decrees? What are happiness and unhappiness other than imagination? What use is the depraved taste of man? Remarkable is his
urge to turn established sayings upside down. Sallust's saying,
"Agreement makes small things grow, but disagreement ruins
large matters," is often praised, but the opposite is rather the
truth! Above this last essay stands: "Only the wise man is happy,"
but the conclusion is "Only fools are happy." The tone is abandoned and teasing; only in the first essay does Holberg attack
accepted opinions and really mean what he says. There he wishes

to revise the conception of godliness. Far too many people are
misled into believing that true godliness is found in the imagin-
ings of visionaries, in the penitent struggles of the melancholy,
and in the gesticulations of habitual Christians. True religion
is to be recognized by its thankfulness to the Creator, severity
to the self, and forebearance toward others.

Holberg wrote these six spritely pieces in an original, argu-
mentative form which brings them close to works of Cicero and
Seneca, and doubtless it was his dealings with these classical
writers, both regularly quoted by Montaigne, that made Holberg
write his paradoxical dissertations in Latin. It was of significance
for Holberg's Danish essays that he began in Latin—soon after-
wards he got the idea of writing *Moral Thoughts* and the sixty-
three chapters of these books were worked in the same carefully
polished and meticulous style as the six Latin forerunners. These
six were translated with admirable terseness and elegance for
the new book.

Holberg also embellished his text with well-chosen borrow-
ings. In one chapter maintaining that the ignorant and inexpert
believe that they know and are able to do everything, whereas
wisdom and knowledge make a man modest, he can support his
thesis with a quotation which is as well chosen as it is elo-
quently rendered: "Nothing can be more apt than the words
of Montaigne: the learned and knowledgeable are in the same
fashion as blades of corn; they stand erect with heads held high
so long as they are empty, but when they come to maturity they
humble themselves and bow their heads." Another passage in
which the author is warning against filling oneself with overmuch learning, he again borrows some similes from Montaigne,
but here, though, he omits to mention his source. "As plants
cannot thrive with a superabundance of water, and a lamp is
extinguished by overmuch oil, so the brain is dulled by too much
reading." As always in Holberg there are many quotations from
Greek and particularly Roman authors.

A specialty of *Moral Thoughts*, however, is his use of proverbs.
In previous and in later works of his, Danish proverbs are few
and far between; that *Moral Thoughts* is full of them is no
doubt due to a deliberate embellishment of the style. He had
read Peder Syv's collection of Danish proverbs, which appeared

in 1682–88, with the intention of inserting a number of sayings into his book. For a few months he soaked his mind in proverbs, and they flow from his pen as he requires them. But he later forgot them. When Holberg translated his Latin essay which sought to prove that happiness and unhappiness are not linked to particular organs, he replaced a quotation from Horace with a proverb from Peter Syv's collection. "While the rich become frail and bowed, the poor are healthy and active, or, as it is said, 'poverty feeds but does not fatten.'"

The aim of *Moral Thoughts* was "to examine accepted opinions and to show how the shadow is taken for the substance and how vices are confused with virtues." But this criticism of prejudices has a practical end in view. Moral philosophy will not only teach its readers respect for the opinion of others, religious and scholarly tolerance, but also how to order their lives to yield greater profit. On Seneca's model Holberg is a practical philosopher of life, a philosophical preacher who wants men to distinguish between the essential and the inessential not only in the selection of objects for scientific study, but also in everyday conduct. In a hortatory chapter he discusses the right use of time and, as is his wont, speaks mainly of errors and abuses. How many superfluous books are printed! How much time is wasted on imprecise speeches by lawyers and on pretentious sermons! At the end of the chapter Holberg warmly applauds a constructive comment which he has found in Seneca: "It is unjust to complain of the brevity of life: it is only a matter of using time aright. When life is full it is long—*longa est vita si plena est.*"

Terse maxims on these lines are the soul of Holberg's *Moral Thoughts*. The fertile paradox is at once form and content of the book. His criticism of instruction in Christianity in the schools is conveyed in sentences designed to shock: "Children must be made into human beings before they become Christians. If anyone learns theology before learning to become a man, he will never become a man." For anyone who, like Holberg, believed in the divine light of reason within, it is the first aim of education to teach pupils to use their senses and their understanding. When they have learned to observe, they will be able to understand the necessity of a Creator and realize the lofty qualities

He must necessarily possess. In the deepest sense Holberg is a man of the Enlightenment.

And this tendency was not to the liking of Christian VI's clergy. When a school was to be inaugurated in Bergen on June 16, 1752, the Bishop, Erik Pontoppidan, held a Latin oration, in which he praised Bergen's famous son, Ludvig Holberg, but warned against reading his writings without a proper theological caution. In Epistle 130 Holberg says that "some in mockery have called his writings a heathen morality." It is certain that in *Moral Thoughts* Holberg was attacking the new Pietistic orthodoxy. Time after time he claims the right and the duty for every man to scrutinize the basis of his faith. His contempt for blind faith knows no bounds. In this book he himself has an unshaken confidence in the enlightened or omniscient Creator "who does nothing to conflict with his justice and goodness." In 1744 Holberg was not yet troubled by religious doubts—these did not arise until later, when the yoke of the Pietists had long since been removed.

While the original six Latin essays had titles, the chapters in *Moral Thoughts* were each headed by one of the Latin epigrams Holberg had published in 1737. In many cases the essay develops the idea contained in the epigram; in others the verse is included for the sake of consistency. There is a tradition for this arrangement. In the English *Spectator* every article was introduced not by a title but with a quotation from a classical author, often a verse from a Roman poet, as a motto. In his Latin epigrams Holberg was cultivating a genre which had been a favorite of the learned in the previous century. In 1737 he published 758 of them divided into five sections or books (libri). Gradually more were added, and in 1749 the epigrammist collected all his 937 small poems into an independent volume entitled *Epigrammatum libri septem*. These short Latin poems are Holberg's lyrics. In its basic form an epigram consists of a distichon, two lines of verse, one of them a hexameter, and the other a pentameter. The first line prepares for the point, which is delivered in the second.

Ex nihilo fit nil, cum dicis, turpiter erras,
Nam te Prætorem fecimus ex nihilo. (Book IV, No. 56)

From nothing nothing comes—in saying this you err,
When we make you, a cipher, into a minister!

Claudia, cum Veneris fit mentio, sæpe rubescit;
Artibus at Veneris nulla perita magis. (Book II, No. 53)

Often blushes Claudia when of Love some words are said,
In the art of Love, however, she seems born and bred.

Holberg's model from ancient Rome, Martial, was mostly a
satirist. Of more recent poets writing in Latin, the Englishman
John Owen, who died in 1622, and the Dane Henrik Harder
(1642–1683) taught Holberg to extend the genre to include
apothegms and self-analysis. When in a French periodical he
read about the Chinese wisdom of Confucius, he took from
there subjects for a number of epigrams whose philosophy is
temperance, satisfaction with one's lot, and patience. Like his
predecessors, Holberg often increases his epigrams to two or
more disticha. Thus, in a self-portrait, the point of which is a
powerful antithesis, there is in this intellectually honed poetry
something in common with the frankness of his autobiography:

Defraudans genium comites facio geniales,
Urbanos risus commoveo ipse dolens.
Fabellas fingo, jocunda poemata scribo,
Atque urbem grato compleo saepe sono.
Verbo ridentes risus exsors facio ipse,
Laetitiam moveo; privor at ipse movens. (Book IV, No. 68)

Deprived of joy myself, I oft make others merry,
Make whole cities laugh, though I myself contrary.
I fashion comedies, shape songs of jocund measure,
With sweetest sound I fill the town with pleasure.
While dull myself, my wit makes others better;
Mirth I beget — for all but its begetter!

CHAPTER 9

The Revival of the Theater

C HRISTIAN VI died on August 6, 1746, and was succeeded by his son, Frederik V, whose gay and festive outlook was already known to everyone. With his young and lovely queen, Louise, the new king was welcomed by the people with joyful expectancy. Holberg immediately dedicated a large work to him, a translation of the late-Greek historian Herodian of Syria, who wrote about the Roman emperors from Marcus Aurelius onwards. The dedication runs: "The King's life-loving regimen has so charmed me and all honest subjects that we have, as it were, been given new life and energy." Holberg praises Frederik V for the twin virtues generally considered incompatible—majesty and benevolence, and in 1748 he praises the new Danish court for its simple yet cultivated manners, which prevailed upon the old philosopher to be present when their majesties were giving audience. "Anyone can attend an elevated gathering here without wearing mask or paint, without carefully measured steps, without flights of eloquence, so that, here in a royal court, the simplicity of natural bearing is presented." "It is indescribable," he says two years later, "with what fervent joy an ordinary man hears Her Majesty, though an English princess, speaking with the royal children in Danish" (Epistle 377).

I Comedies Again

When the year of mourning was over, public entertainments could be considered once more, and cultural life began to blossom forth again. There was competition for permission to open a theater in Copenhagen, and, obviously on Holberg's recommendation, on December 30 C. A. Thielo, an organist, was granted a charter for a Danish theater. Thielo mustered a group of actors, among them a brilliant comedian Gert Londemann, in a hall

108

belonging to Christian Berg, a restaurateur, where a theater was equipped, and on April 14, 1747, the Danish actors inaugurated their repertoire of comedies by performing *The Political Tinker*. But the auditorium was too small, and after 1747 the actors were granted royal permission to perform in Tjærehuset, a kind of armory near what is now Kongens Nytorv (The King's New Square). But as this building was soon to be demolished to give place to a specially-built theater building, in 1748 the comedians moved to their third location: a theater in the street called Store Kongensgade. Here, Julius von Qvoten, a son of Holberg's old rival between November, 1747, and May, 1748, implemented his right to present Danish and German comedies until he had to close down for lack of support. The troupe of Danish actors remained here until the fine new theater, erected by the royal architect, Nicolai Eigtved, could be inaugurated on December 18, 1748, the queen's birthday.

During all these moves from one temporary stage to another, Holberg had been working closely with the troupe. He undoubtedly supported the actors when, in the course of the summer, they made Thielo resign from the management and took over the license themselves. Holberg had great influence on the repertoire and on the casting. He operated both as dramatic adviser and as talent scout. As late as May 17, 1753, in a sharp letter he had to reproach the actors for their behavior toward a newly appointed actress. Several of Holberg's *Epistles* (1748 ff.) arose from his practical connection with the theater. He wished his own comedies to be performed and then plays by Molière, Regnard, and others, but he was violently opposed when a more recent, lighter taste began to appear. Epistle 495 is, so to speak, Holberg's speech as an advocate, giving grounds for the theater to perform a French play, *La vie est un songe* by Louis de Boissy: in spite of some absurdities in it, it did contain a coherent action and gay scenes. The play was performed from March, 1753. In other Epistles Holberg gives his impressions after the performance. As a theater critic he was especially hard on Destouches, whose subtle psychology and fine comedy he finds to be without logic and coherence, pure confusion.

After the new theater had really got under way Holberg wrote several new plays for it. He favored philosophical comedy. *Plutus* is designed to prove that the benefit of riches is most happily distributed when Plutus, the god of wealth, is blind. Plutus and his counterpart, Penea, are personifications of riches and poverty. Even more abstract is the female title figure in the comedy *The Republic*. She is the state, *res publica*, plagued by advocates of wild schemes, and has to take an emetic to be rid of them. In these abstract figures there is a certain link with the originator of European comedy, Aristophanes. Drawing on the philosophical history of antiquity, in his two comedies *The Imaginary Philosopher* and *Sganarel's Journey* Holberg makes fun of the remote philosopher. Above all, Holberg is very strongly attracted by ancient times. *The Ghost or Abracadabra* is an energetic version in a local setting of Plautus's *Mostelaria*: while Jeronimus has been away on his journeys his son and his servant have been enjoying themselves. Then Jeronimus unexpectedly turns up again and Henrik tries to make him imagine that a murdered man is haunting the house. But the truth will out one day. As this comedy had only male roles, Holberg wrote another play, *The Transformed Bridegroom*, for women only. Among the comedies of Holberg's old age *Plutus* especially was successful when it was performed in April, 1751, and in subsequent years. Holberg was proud that a philosophical comedy could please the public, but he doubtless also realized that this was partly due to the colorful procession of characters in the comedy. Holberg was against costume pieces, but he explains that in *Plutus* the decor speaks to the mind as much as to the eye (Epistle 447).

II *The* Epistles

Holberg purposely gave *Moral Thoughts* a unified character. Throughout, the style was carefully studied and a critical individualistic attitude marked almost all the chapters. In the *Epistles* Holberg realized that he must not decorate the style so much and that the subject matter was much more varied. The title page states that the *Epistles* touch upon political science, metaphysics, morality, and philosophy, and sometimes contain lighthearted matter. In them Holberg is making a book reflecting his shifting interests and concerns. Whenever an event or a writing arouses thoughts within him, he composes an article about it and assigns it a number. These fictitious letters are introduced with "To * *" and close with "I remain, etc." But between these two phrases there is little suggestion of the fictional correspondents. One letter is, however, addressed to a real recipient. In his preface to *Herodian* (1746) Holberg had urged Danish students to translate Greek and Latin authors into Danish. Several took up his challenge, and among them was the young historian Peter Frederik Suhm, who in 1749 published a volume of military science translated from Greek and Latin. In Epistle 439 Holberg thanks the translator without mentioning him by name. He praises Suhm because he would rather obtain for himself thorough knowledge at home than clumsy gallantries in foreign parts. "You, sir, advance along the road leading to the true goal and will therefore become one of our country's most capable men. I remain, etc." Suhm was later to become an important Danish historiographer. In the *Epistles* Holberg is, in effect, keeping a journal of his opinions. The first two volumes were published in 1748 and contain Nos. 1–183, the next two volumes, of 1750, and contain 184–446, and the fifth and final volume was published posthumously in 1754; it contains Nos. 447–539.

Holberg's religious views were not constant. We can trace the stages through which they pass from his stay in Paris in 1714–15, when he was aroused to criticize Catholicism. Then in 1728, in the first part of his autobiography, he tells of some authors who, some years before, had made him doubt whether the Bible was literally God's Word. Worst of all was Richard Simon, a Catholic, who not openly but secretly attacked revelation. Simon was one of the founders of biblical criticism. He went further than the Catholic Church thought seemly and some of his books were placed on the Index. Holberg, however, overcame his doubts about the divine origin of the Bible, and he was not even troubled by Bayle's doubts about the justice of God.

Pierre Bayle (1647–1706) had been born in France, but on account of his critical opinions he worked mostly in Holland, where his writings were published during the last twenty years of his life. He applied his intellectual powers to attacking popular superstitions and religious intolerance. In his great *Dictionary* of historical personages, Bayle hints boldly that the good and the evil which occur in the world can be explained only if it is assumed, as did the Manicheans in Persia of old, that the world originates from two divinities, the Father of Light and the Father of Darkness. Bayle was contradicted by many: in 1710 the German philosopher Gottfried Wilhelm Leibniz (1646–1716) published in French a detailed counterblast to Bayle's ideas: *Théodicée*, i.e., a defense of the justice of God. The world created by God cannot be perfect, for then it would be God itself, but among the infinite possibilities available to God, He created the best. This view was shared by Holberg in 1737 when in a couple of epigrams he maintained that both evil and good must belong to the created world: there would be nothing good if there were nothing evil (Book II, No. 94). To anyone who enquires how there can be so much evil if God exists, we must reply: If there were no God, how could there then be so much good (III, No. 78). And in *Moral Thoughts* Holberg maintains that if God had created man without sin he would then have been without free will, not man but a mere machine. Just as Leibniz does, Holberg differentiates between metaphysical, physical, and moral evil in the world and seeks to demonstrate that these evils have their clearly defined significance. But when we come to 1748, and thus to the first volume of the *Epistles*, the tone has changed. A more profound study of Bayle has obviously opened his eyes to further aspects of the matter and greater problems. He has realized that his own arguments were plausible but did not untie the knot. The result is that he abandons a final solution. The problem of evil is subdivided into several problems, and Holberg seeks to find a satisfactory answer to each of them. That the angels are free must be because they, in contrast to men, have passed the test (Epistle 1). He finds it very difficult to reconcile the fate of the human race with the thought of God's omniscience and justice (Epistles 26, 28, 178). Yet in his epistles of the third and fourth volumes he is obliged to abandon even this cautious defense. By this time he will only admit that the *Théodicée* of Leibniz has not countered the criticism of Bayle and that many regard the greatest opponent of Bayle as having achieved nothing (Epistles 320 and 322). Holberg thus sees no other possibility than keeping to revelation, according to which all that God created was good and all the evil we now see in the world flows from the misdeed of our first parents by which man became subject to vices, diseases, and death, and the whole world became cursed and lost the glory with which it had been endowed at the original creation.

We find Holberg's view of the practical meaning of Christianity in Epistle 46, a proposed moral catechism. In this Epistle Holberg gathers the reflections of many years; it can be seen that his principles incline in various directions. Viewed rightly, this Epistle is an important documentation of the religious and ethical debate of the century. When, in the first article of his catechism, Holberg maintains that the world owes its origin to a creator, he is then attacking those who deny God, the atheists, who, according to *Moral Thoughts,* were "dangerous in a state, because they do not fear God's punishment." It is obvious, says the second article, that God must be worshiped, i.e., thanked for His care. In another passage Holberg develops the theme that the worship of God consists primarily of work and "one hour's meditation on the improvement of life is better than a whole year of morning and evening prayers" (Epistle 336). It is clear, we are taught in the third article, that the injustice to be seen in the world must be put right in the next, where penalties and rewards are awarded according to merit. The fourth article says that nothing should be believed that is contrary to the ordinary senses of men, otherwise we fall away to the superstition of the Catholics that the bread and wine of the Lord's Supper are transmuted into the flesh and blood of Christ (*Moral Thoughts*). We must, says the fifth article, shun all learning that undermines God's goodness, justice, and therefore we must not put our trust in the Calvinists, who believe that from eternity past God has predestined some to salvation, others to perdition. And finally the sixth article is directed against the Pietists and other "enthusiasts" who "lay upon us not to hate or persecute anyone who errs against his will." In Holberg's *Epistles* the serious and didactic tone is undoubtedly dominant, but a certain playfulness also finds a place. While defending some historical characters otherwise vulnerable, e.g., Cardinal Fleury (Epistle 13) and Pope Gregory VII (Epistle 61), he finds occasion to write *An Apology for*

the Devil (Epistle 60) and we shall quote this here in its entirety
as a representative of the *Epistles*.

AN APOLOGY FOR THE DEVIL

To * *

Our last conversation concerned apologies, or writings of defense,
and I expressed my dislike of them, both because an honorable man
and a good writing need no apology, for the conduct of the man
and the contents of the writing may be left to defend themselves;
and also because it is possible to write apologies for anything, even
indeed for the Devil. You laughed at these words of mine, and said
that this would indeed be difficult. I rejoined that it would not be
more difficult to write than the apology for the ass, in which several
heroic qualities are ascribed to this beast. To show that it is feasible,
I will briefly outline what an apologist who strives to show things
in the best light might cite in defense of the Devil. I shall not speak
of his faculties and understanding because everyone, even his worst
enemies, agrees that a person who has almost 6,000 years behind him
and has thus lived twice as long as the Shoemaker of Jerusalem
must certainly possess more learning and wisdom than all the Seven
Sages of Greece — perhaps even than all the professors in the world
even if molded into one. Unless, of course, it is claimed that he is
becoming childish with age, but no one can say that without maligning
him, since the most learned theologians who have closely studied the
qualities of this gentleman and know him in every fine point, tell us
that he is yet in full vigor, so that age has left but little mark upon
him. Those learned men of the previous century who had the honor
of speaking to the Shoemaker of Jerusalem testified that this same
shoemaker has yet his full five senses, lacking nothing either in understanding or memory, although he has now been wandering around
the world for 1,600 years. There can therefore be no dispute about
the mental faculties and learning of the Devil, which, in view of his
advanced age, cannot be other than great. And it is for this reason
that the Norwegians honor him with the venerable title of Old Erik.
But let us examine the vices ascribed to him. The Devil is said to be
constantly astir to cast men into misfortune and to lead souls astray,
but since he quite plainly and as if by manifesto has declared war
upon the human race, he is more to be excused than many human
beings who, under the guise of friendship, ensnare their neighbors;
who conclude peace and alliances and immediately break them; who
call God to witness the sincerity of their hearts when they are full of
hatred, enmity, and rapacity. Therefore it is said that one may beware

of the Devil but not of men. And he seeks to beguile souls merely in order to strengthen his power and prove that he is a wily politician, statesman, and economist. In pacts and contracts he behaves more uprightly than most men. For when men conclude agreements, they break them at once, bringing themselves into such discredit that none dare rely upon their words unless it be confirmed by the guarantees of others; but experience teaches us that the Devil observes his agreements to the last jot and meticulously fulfills what he has promised to the contracting parties, attacking no one before the stipulated time. This is seen in the cases of Dr. Faustus and other worthy men, whom, by virtue of contracts entered into, he has either instructed in arts, learning, and political science, or has aided with large subventions of money, demanding no payment *pro labore* until the final hour of the stipulated time had arrived. Among all the evil things that are said about the Devil one never hears any charge of breach of contract, nor of his defrauding anyone with counterfeit coins or false goods, as our merchants and writers are wont to do nowadays, the former by giving their wares false designations, and the latter by giving their works misleading titles in order to attract advance orders for them. But the Devil, for his part, fulfills his obligations, demanding nothing in advance, and so one never hears of anyone who makes a compact with the Devil demanding any guarantee—an infallible proof that he keeps his contracts punctiliously! To this it may be objected that the Devil's honorable conduct does not arise from basic honesty but from self-interest, since he thereby furthers his profession and entices others to enter into contracts with him. But I wonder whether our so-called honest merchants are really honest in their trade and their conduct merely for the sake of being honest. Does not the uprightness that they practice flow from the same source? It is said that when two men do the same thing, it may not be the same thing after all. For what is called a virtue in these merchants is, in the Devil, depicted as a major vice. Then the Devil, having once been given an evil reputation, finds that fornication, murder, robbery, theft, and all other wicked deeds are ascribed to his inspiration. I do not venture to acquit him completely, although I maintain that the general reproaches cast upon the Devil have evil effects and are ill-founded. Evil effects, because, in this way, sinners shrug off their guilt and use the Devil as a cover for their misdeeds. And ill-based, because, without any cooperation from without, depraved flesh and blood is capable of driving to sin. The tale is told that once, in the Old Market Square, the Devil met a girl who had allowed herself to be seduced and was approaching confinement. He came up to her and said, "How now, my good Martha, it seems that you have committed a folly!" To which the girl replied with a sigh, "Alas, how the Devil doth moil!" The

Devil, knowing himself to be quite guiltless in the matter, flushed angrily and boxed her ears soundly, saying, "Take that for your lying mouth! The whole blame lies in your own lusty flesh, for neither I nor my mother have had the least part in it." Further, it is said that the Devil disquiets men by nocturnal haunting. But a conception of the Devil appropriate to a cunning and malevolent spirit has caused me to be of another opinion than the learned on this question—partly, indeed, because I have found no good reason for him to do this, unless we are to assume that old age has driven him to childishness (which no one will admit), but partly because by such haunting he would be acting against his own interests. But such an opinion being reckoned as a vice on my part, I have relinquished it, and I now profess with the orthodox that it really is the Devil who haunts at night churchyards, houses, and nurseries, but, the result of such haunting being to make people god-fearing, such nocturnal activity shows the Devil as a friend rather than an adversary of mankind. So that this, far from being ascribed to him as a vice, should be reckoned in his favor. His office, which consists of being the tormentor or executioner of the damned, ought not to sully his name or reputation, for it is a necessity. Just as a city cannot do without its executioner, so the human race cannot dispense with such an executioner-in-chief to carry out the sentences passed upon the guilty. The office is, then, not only in itself necessary, but even an honorable one. Indeed, one sees that the ancient Greeks had no hesitation in making two highly esteemed men, Minos and Rhadamanthus, the executioners in the kingdom of Pluto. From this it is plain that the Devil is not as black as he is painted. On the contrary, he has many good qualities, so that it is less difficult to compose an apology for him than for many men whose deficiencies cannot be glossed over. Many impartial men have doubtless noticed that condemnations of him have gone too far, and probably if the learned and impartial theologian Gottfried Arnold, who pleaded the cause of hated men, had lived somewhat longer, he would have taken upon himself the task of composing an apology for this notorious spirit. And the task is thus proved not to be so difficult but that with the assistance of some good rhetoric it can at least be made presentable. This may be said with certainty: many of those who mock the Devil, especially those who depict him with horns on his brow, have little honor behind their words, for he can turn their own mockery upon them by bidding them feel their own brows. It may, too, be reckoned among his good qualities that he bears his horns with more patience than most men, who demean themselves with lawsuits and summonses. For in well-nigh 6,000 years no one has ever heard of the Devil accusing anyone in the matrimonial court. Which proves that even if he is a cuckold, he is a sensible cuckold who knows how to conceal his ignominy better than most men. That the Devil tempts men there can scarcely be. any doubt, but as experience shows that the Devil's so-called temptations have been exorcised with powders and drops, it is evidence that these charges are often very ill-founded. Unless it be maintained that devils can be driven out with crab's-eyes or purgatives, which is to take too mean a view of one's adversary. So there you have a defense of the Devil written in haste. You may draw your own conclusions from it as to what a clever disputer might make of it who undertook to defend his case in public debate, or an advocate who has achieved a reputation for making a bad case good. Logic and rhetoric are the two chief sciences, for with the help of logic Zeno proved that nothing in the world moves, and with logic Erasmus Montanus proved that Per the Parish Clerk was a cockerel and that it was a merit to strike one's parents. But to speak seriously, I ask you not to show this letter to anybody, particularly not to Reverend Niels or to Per the Parish Clerk, for they would explain everything literally and make of it texts for sermons. Then I might fare like a certain man who was made a cardinal in the Merry Papal College founded in this city some time since. In his estate some papers were discovered in which he was styled Cardinal Orsini. The chancery officers, taking this literally, deliberated with the county court as to whether the deceased could be permitted Christian burial.

I remain, etc.

It will be plain from this quotation that the author of *Peder Paars* was still writing in the *Epistles*. Another example is Epistle 193 in which he parodies the Swedish historian Olof Rudbeck, who in 1679 had published an immense work entitled *Atlantica* to prove that the island of Atlantis, which Plato believed to have sunk beneath the sea, was in fact Sweden. In his work *The History of the Kingdom of Sweden* (1747), the Swedish author Olof Dalin had sharply criticized Rudbeck and in his Epistle Holberg, Dalin's Danish kindred spirit, mocks at the historical phantasies of the previous century. The new critical spirit is campaigning against the dreams of national greatness to be found in Sweden and Denmark.

In the *Epistles* we are reminded too of Holberg the comedy writer, and not only because there is plenty of mention of his comedies. In the English *Spectator*, which Holberg probably read in an abridged French translation, he found the framework for Epistle 12, which he fills out with his own bright ideas. In the *Spectator* he had seen the theme developed that there are pedants to be found in all walks of life and not only among scholars. There are court pedants, martial pedants, legal hairsplitters, and statesmen who can speak only of politics. In his Epistle Holberg sketches five characters, namely the pedant scholar and the four just mentioned. In these exceedingly funny Epistles the anecdote is his strong point. A schoolmaster had once to call upon a courtier. He was made to wait for half an hour before he was granted audience because My Lord was standing before the mirror curling his hair. The schoolmaster grew impatient and departed, muttering to himself, "What a high-born pedant!" When at last, after much care and attention, My Lord had achieved the desired symmetry of his hair, arranging it according to the rules of geometry, he called to his servant, "Show that pedant in!"

Holberg was never tired of looking at the bizarre aspects of human nature. The psychological formula of his comedies was chaotic man, and this was also the basis of a number of his Epistles. In Bayle's *Dictionary* he read one day about a distinguished unmarried lady in ancient Greece, Hipparchia, who fell in love with a philosopher called Crates, who belonged to the school of Cynics, or dog philosophers, and who, in accordance with the principles of his sect, was living in dirt and poverty. Hipparchia married Crates and followed him in all the practical consequences of his philosophy. This story calls to Holberg's mind the story of a Danish noblewoman who had first found satisfaction in marriage with a coarse man of the humblest class, and, says Holberg, "I have heard this from her own mouth, when I was at her house, which was at a ferry crossing in Falster, after her husband had been arrested for some misdeed." This was Marie Grubbe, and it was this Epistle that inspired J. P. Jacobsen (1847–1885) to insert the profound conversation between her and Holberg in the last chapter of his novel *Marie Grubbe* (English translation. *Marie Grubbe*, A Lady of the Seventeenth Century. New York. 1917 and 1962). In Epistle 89 Holberg conceives these two ladies of rank who fell in love with indigent suitors as being examples of the corrupt state of humanity. In many respects man is still an animal who defies definition.

III   Moral Fables

In this section we must also make mention of Holberg's *Moral Fables,* which were published in 1751. These comprise 232 tales with themes to be found elsewhere throughout Holberg's works. According to the laws of the genre, in most of the *Fables* the human types are given animal forms. Once, when the wolf employed the ass as a physician and became even more sick during the "cure," he sued the ass, but the judge, the lion, took the view that the wolf ought to bear the costs of the case for employing a doctor whom he knew to be an ass. The style of these fables is dry, the tone cool, the attitude to human beings exceedingly skeptical. A mole asked a beaver, who was a servant at court, what was said about him at the lion's court. To which the beaver replied, "I have not been able to observe that anyone in the whole court knows that such creatures as moles exist." (Fable 192, with the ironical title *The Arrogance of the Mole.*) In a long and strange fable we hear about the mites who assume that their cheese is the whole world and worship two gods, Margrethe, the milkmaid, who has created their world, and Glirus the rat who nibbles the cheese. From this it can be seen, the fable points out, that the doctrine of two independent principles of good and evil is older than the Manicheans. Such pessimism is not, however, the only attitude of the fables. In two connected tales of *Moral Fables* the fabulist seeks to show that when the two powers of religion and reason form an alliance then their enemies, unbelief (atheism) and superstition (religious fanaticism) can accomplish nothing (181–82).

Moral Fables was not the last book Holberg published. After the success of *Niels Klim* abroad and the translations of the historical writings, etc., Holberg regarded himself not only as a Scandinavian literary figure who learned from the great literatures, but also as a European writer who took part in cultural discussions on the highest level. In 1748 Montesquieu's epoch-making work *De l'Esprit des Lois* was published. In this Montesquieu used his genius to analyze three forms of government: despotism, monarchy, and democracy. Few books have had such a lasting success as Montesquieu's *L'Esprit des Lois,* and in part it was a *succès de scandale.* Immediately after it was published there appeared critical reviews of it and short polemical works in reply to it. Interest in the subject was so great that the booksellers were able to bind the various articles together into small volumes. Holberg decided to mingle his protesting voice with the others. In rather fanciful French he wrote a little book which was published in Copenhagen in 1753 and entitled *Remarques sur quelques positions qui se trouvent dans L'Esprit des Lois.* It goes without saying that Holberg recognized Montesquieu's work as a masterpiece. He admired especially and unreservedly his two sections on religion, and he intended to make Danish translations of them, but he never got any further with this project than to translate the thirteenth chapter of Book XXV. In 1660, as we have seen, a *coup d'état* directed against the nobility had established absolutism in Denmark. From that time the king had to look to the clergy and the upper middle classes for support and, later, to the new nobility that had arisen from these two classes. There is no doubt that Holberg was a convinced and sincere supporter of the new regime, which had certainly made his own career easier. In 1747 he bequeathed to the state all his lands, and these were compounded into a barony. From then on Holberg was a baron, and it was with this title that he signed his *Remarques* on Montesquieu.

Holberg had been watching the course of another revolution which made a great impression upon him. This was the transformation of Russia brought about by Peter the Great, who died in 1725. Russia provided Holberg with clear evidence that the fortunes of a state are essentially the work of its ruler. For this reason he protests against Montesquieu's theory that climate can mold the character of a nation. He has frequently observed both in his study of history and in his consideration of contemporary events that the inhabitants of a country have changed in temperament, although the climate of the country has remained the same. He therefore concludes that it is the laws of the land, the system of government, and the sovereign that shape the soul of a nation.

In general the critics were outraged by Montesquieu's principle that virtue was to be found only in a democracy. Most of them misunderstood the sense in which Montesquieu used the expression "political virtue," that is, love of one's fatherland, or more precisely love of the laws of one's country. Holberg perhaps makes this concept seem a little too closely allied to heroic patriotism when, against Montesquieu's theory, he advances the historical example of the Romans:

At the beginning these people were governed by kings whose power was limited by the laws. This is what the writer calls a monarchy, the driving principle of which is not virtue but ambition. But we learn from history that the Romans never showed so much virtue, so many heroic qualities, and so many proofs of the love they bore their country, as they did under that very monarchy, in which the princes by their uprightness, their justice, their understanding of affairs, their ability in the art of government, and in exercising all virtues, made themselves loved by their subjects, whom they encouraged by their example to value the safety of their city higher than their own lives. The abolition of kingship did not at first abate this former virtue, for the system of government was in reality the same, the power of the king having been transferred to two consuls. But as the form of government came closer to democracy, the old qualities began to vanish; love of the fatherland was changed into love of one's self, dutiful respect for superiors into arrogance. The meanest citizen came to regard himself as a man of importance, and since each man had a part in the government of the land, the populace treated state officials and the commanders of the army as the works of their own hands. But I will be asked whether I have properly understood the author's contention that corruption in a democracy is followed by serious consequences. He wishes to speak only of a healthy democracy, in which virtue, being at the helm, shows itself to a high degree and sheds its light with greater brightness. But I reply to this that it is nothing but an ideal Platonic republic that has never existed and can never exist, for a state is not made up of angels, but of men who are by nature weak and defective, and they themselves recognize that it is nothing but a vain dream to hope to live in peace and security under the regime of complete freedom. . . . I admit [he adds further on] that freedom is an inestimable treasure, but since such freedom can scarcely be combined with perfect security, it is but an imaginary benefit.

In his conclusion Holberg returns to the importance of the personality of the ruler to his subjects: "It can be said that all government is good when he who governs possesses good qualities and history demonstrates that a people can very well be just as happy and sometimes less oppressed [i.e., by taxes, etc.] under an arbitrary government than in a free state. Our kings here in Denmark, since being invested with unlimited power, bear witness to this fact."

In all absolutist countries Montesquieu was suspect because of the way he tacitly equated despotism and absolute monarchy. "I do not know," writes Holberg, "what our illustrious author means by despotic government in which neither virtue nor honor can have a function. If by despotism he means all arbitrary governments, which seems to be his opinion, he is speaking contrary to experience. There are numerous examples to be found in history of those whom he terms despots who were full of wisdom and integrity."

In this work Holberg is certainly playing the part of an advocate; he is defending Danish absolutism. But it is also true that in attacking Montesquieu by referring to historical examples he is attacking him on his weakest flank. He is playing the historian's experience against the philosopher's generalizations. His attack on Montesquieu appeared on October 1, 1753, and Holberg died four months later on January 28, 1754. The wise old man's mind did not fail him and right to the end he possessed the courage and the ability to enter into a debate with the most intelligent Frenchman of his century.

CHAPTER 10

Sorø Academy

E VEN during Holberg's lifetime he exerted considerable
influence in many fields. We have seen him writing
comedies when a new theater was in need of them, and we
have observed his resoluteness when the same theater was being
reestablished. Holberg was endowed with both creative talent
and, most fortunately, the practical sense that art also requires.
This fertile writer was a shrewd businessman. Like Voltaire, he
belonged to the new generation of professional authors. Their
books were not issued at the expense of a wealthy patron, but,
like any other commodity, were on the market to make money
for their creator. There was a readership, new and with pur-
chasing power, not only for Holberg's popular historical and
juridical works, but for *Peder Paars* and the comedies. In the
author's preface to the first volume of Hans Mickelsen's
comedies, Holberg wrote that it was not to be construed as
parsimony that he did not give away his books. Since he wrote
frequently, he was to be regarded just as any other tradesmen,
who were not usually willing to give away their own goods.
Having so many acquaintances made it invidious to give to one
without also giving to another. And he concludes gaily: the
trade might otherwise go bankrupt. In Trondhjem Holberg
had a dealer, Aage Hagen, who kindly sold *Peder Paars* and the
comedies for him; in a letter about the first volume of the
comedies Holberg assures him: "You will get laughter in plenty
for your 2½ marks."

Holberg was most often his own publisher, and even book-
seller: his works were sold from his own residence. Seeing that
he also received a professor's salary and lived unmarried and
spartanly, it is no cause for surprise that by around 1730 he
had amassed a fortune, which he invested in property in

123

Copenhagen and, later, in manor houses in Zealand; in 1740 he bought the estate of Brorup near Slagelse and in 1745 that of Tersløsegaard near Sorø. The University of Copenhagen put Holberg's business acumen to good use in 1737 when it elected him quaestor, i.e. bursar, and from that time he was relieved of lecturing duties. In 1735 he made known publicly that the money he had made or would come to make from his writings "I intend to return to the public in the form of a useful foundation for the further advancement of the Danish language." It was therefore a natural and happy idea to request him to support the reestablishment of Sorø Academy. In great measure Sorø Academy promoted the new kind of education advocated by Holberg.

In 1565 Herluf Trolle had founded the school of Herlufsholm, modeled on the learned schools of Saxony, and in the same way Frederik II had established a school in 1568 at Frederiksborg, and this was removed to Sorø in 1586. This existed there until 1737, and from 1623 to 1665 it was supplemented on a higher level by an academy for young noblemen, which had the same rights as the University of Copenhagen. It was this latter academy that was reestablished in 1747 and functioned until 1794. To this academy Holberg bequeathed his estates, which at the same time were designated the Barony of Holberg. By becoming a baron Holberg achieved an annual tax saving of 300 rix-dollars, and he was able to add this to his capital. In 1751, three years before his death, Holberg made over the interest on the capital to the academy, as the money proved to be necessary for the running of the academy, which then showed its gratitude by granting Holberg a tomb in the old and distinguished abbey church.

There can be no doubt that Holberg exerted an influence when the statutes of Sorø Academy were being framed. Count Heinrich Reuss, who was prefect of the county of Sorø, was the leading spirit in founding the new academy. It was probably he who made approaches to Holberg, and there exist in copy "some reflexions" that Holberg sent to Count Reuss and which in part reappear in Epistle 177. It was one of Holberg's main themes that young people should be educated in their native land and "incredible sums of money" thus be saved. Holberg, who in his younger years had had his share of the roving spirit he now wished to combat, had grown incurious about conditions abroad, so much so indeed that in Epistle 447 he says that if Constantinople lay on the island of Funen he would weigh up whether to make the journey. So it is not difficult to trace Holberg's reflexions in the founding statutes of the academy, for they state that no one may be permitted to travel abroad before he has studied for three years in Sorø or Copenhagen. In 1749, when Holberg published a new edition of his *Description of Denmark and Norway*, a new chapter was added dealing with the academy for noblemen at Sorø and in this the statutes were included *in extenso*. It was really the beginning of a new age. There were to be no learned disputations, except for those students who desired them. On ceremonial occasions, however, the students were to take turns in making speeches in Danish, Latin, German, or French "so that the young men may accustom themselves to speaking publicly with grace and to some purpose." And then, too, they were to be assigned subjects for "all kinds of letters, stories, or narratives." The lectures were generally to be in Danish, and they were to be public. In *Moral Thoughts* Holberg had propounded that the professors of the university, instead of giving lectures, "at certain times and places should present themselves in order to answer the questions that were put to them by the young students ... and to explain to them what they were unable to understand in the books and writings to read which they had been previously recommended." This demand recurs in Holberg's reflexions, ·and the statutes lay down that the professors are to hold question hours with the students and if the questions cannot be solved at once, the answering is to be postponed so that the teachers may have "occasion and desire" to look into the matter. Once again we think of Holberg when the statutes lay down that "for the use of the students a number of the best foreign newspapers should be taken." Professors of political science are to make excerpts from them for the students and comment upon the information so that "the young men become accustomed to speaking with modesty and caution about what concerns foreign powers."

Even though Sorø Academy did not have the crucial importance for the education of state officials that had been envisaged, it is important to note Holberg's relationship to it. Time and again Holberg's common sense and creative criticism have been of use to his dual fatherland. Holberg's work is not only the flower of the Age of Enlightenment in Scandinavia, he is a living force, an encouragement and support every time destructive forces in nature or history are impeding true progress. Holberg will never become superfluous, for the threat of disaster is always hanging over mankind's head.

On All Saint's Day, November 1, 1755, the year after Holberg's death, a fearful disaster did occur. Lisbon was struck by an earthquake that lasted for nine minutes. When the tremors had subsided, three quarters of the city had been devastated. The earthquake cost 30,000 lives. The news spread all over Europe, and it was reported that over 100,000 people had been buried under their houses, and this was how it was reported by a Copenhagen newspaper on December 8, 1755.

By its suddenness and its extent the disaster shocked men's minds and provoked comments from both Pietists and Rationalists. In 1756 Holberg's younger contemporary, Bishop Brorson of Ribe, whose hymns and spiritual songs we have already encountered, issued a long poem in alexandrines, *Lissabons ynkelige Undergang* (The Pitiful Perishing of Lisbon), in which, taking newspapers, etc. as his sources, he sketched the earthquake and its effects. The poet-preacher exhorts all to learn from the harsh speech of God: Lisbon was a Christian city and its devastation was a warning to Christendom; would that other great cities heed the significance of this unparalleled scourge. Brorson is most concerned for those so-called Christians who can see traces of God the Creator everywhere in nature, but cannot find God Himself; those who believe that they have rest in their soul without having found Christ. Here the Pietist is speaking of the Deists, the adherents of the religiosity of reason. In the same year one of these worshipers of human understanding, Voltaire, published a poem, likewise in alexandrines, *La Destruction de Lisbonne* (later reworked under the title of *Le Désastre de Lisbonne*). In this poem Voltaire brandished his fist at the Almighty who allowed a disaster of such magnitude: if there had to be an earthquake, He did not need to let it occur in a populous city, but could have sited it in the middle of the desert. "I respect my God, but I love the universe," says the poet, and continues: "Evil is present everywhere on earth; is this due to a good God? God has visited the world of men once, but has not changed it. Couldn't He? or wouldn't He? What is left for us mortals to do? We must suffer, resign ourselves in silence, worship, and die:

> Que faut-il! o Mortels! mortels il faut souffrir,
> Se soumettre en silence, adorer et mourir.

The earthquake in Lisbon made Voltaire doubt progress in the world. In 1759 he published his renowned novel *Candide or Optimism*. In this the author leads his honest, childishly naive hero around the world, including devastated Lisbon. Candide has been brought up to believe in the optimistic teaching of Leibniz that we live in the best possible world. Undeservedly, Candide falls victim to all manner of misfortunes, but without disputing with Providence the patient man, at the close of the novel, finds rest in the thought that "we must cultivate our garden."

The Lisbon earthquake obliged all thinking people to reconsider their convictions. This natural disaster marks a watershed in the century. Its far-reaching consequences make it comparable to the dropping of the atomic bomb on Hiroshima. The smoke of Lisbon about which Brorson wrote was to brood long over the Europe of Holberg and Voltaire.

Selected Bibliography

PRIMARY SOURCES

A detailed description of editions and translations of Holberg's writings is to be found in H. Ehrencron-Müller: *Forfatterlexikon omfattende Danmark, Norge og Island indtil 1814*, Vol. X–XII. Copenhagen. 1933–35.

Some Editions of Holberg's Works

The monumental edition of *Samlede Skrifter*, edited by Carl S. Petersen, Vols. I–XVIII, Copenhagen, 1913–63, presents a reprinting of the original editions as well as, in Vol. XVIII (mainly edited by F. J. Billeskov Jansen and Aage Hansen), critical apparatus and variants in editions from Holberg's lifetime. However, no notes or comments are included in this edition.

With comprehensive comments have appeared, edited by F. J. Billeskov Jansen, *Moralske Tanker*, Copenhagen, 1943; *Memoirer*, Copenhagen, 1943, 2nd ed., 1963; *Epistler*, Vols. I–VIII, Copenhagen, 1944–54.

For a wider public the following two selections have been produced: *Festudgaven*, in six vols. Copenhagen, 1923–25, comprising: *Peder Paars og Skæmtedigtene*, edited by Georg Christensen; *Comoedierne* I–III, edited by Carl Roos; *Niels Klim og Levnetsbrevene*, edited by S. P. Thomas and A. H. Winsnes; *Epistler og Smaastykker i Udvalg*, edited by Francis Bull. This meritorious edition is now very hard to come by.

Værker i Tolv Bind, edited with introduction and comments by F. J. Billeskov Jansen, Copenhagen, 1969–71, is made up as follows: Vol. I: *Natur- og Folkeret*. II: *Peder Paars og Skæmtedigtene*. III–VII: *Komedier* (complete). VIII: *Økonomi og Historie*. IX: *Niels Klim & Moralske Fabler*. X: *Epigrammer og Moralske Tanker*. XI: *Epistler*. XII: *Memoirer & Breve*. This edition is furnished with 600 illustrations shedding light on Holberg's life and literary work.

Holberg's Works in English Translation

See Elias Bredsdorff: *Danish Literature in English Translation. A Bibliography*. Copenhagen. 1950.

Special mention may be made of the following:

1. Autobiography

Holberg's Latin autobiography was published in English translation as *Memoirs of Lewis Holberg. Written by himself in Latin, and now first translated into English.* London. 1827. This translation has now been reprinted as *Memoirs. An eighteenth-century Danish contribution to international understanding.* Edited by Stewart E. Frazer. With 31 illustrations and a portfolio of 33 engravings. Leiden. 1970.

2. Peder Paars

Peter Paars, Canto I. Freely translated from the Danish of Ludvig Holberg by J. H. Sharman. London. 1862.
Peter Paars, Canto II. Freely translated from the Danish of Ludvig Holberg by J. H. Sharman. London. 1862.

Now a complete translation of Peder Paars exists:

Peder Paars. Translated from the Danish by Bergliot Stromsoe. Introduction by Børge Gedsø Madsen. The University of Nebraska Press and The American-Scandinavian Foundation. Lincoln. 1962.

3. Comedies

Of Holberg's comedies sixteen are available in English translation in the following five selections:

Three Comedies [Henry and Pernilla, Captain Bombastes Thunderton, Scatterbrains], translated from the Danish by Lieut. Colonel H. W. L. Hime. Longmans & Co. London. 1912.
Comedies [Jeppe of the Hill, The Political Tinker, Erasmus Montanus], translated from the Danish by O. J. Campbell and Frederic Schenck, with an introduction by O. J. Campbell. Scandinavian Classics, Vol. I, The American-Scandinavian Foundation. New York. 1915.
Four Plays by Holberg [The Fussy Man, The Masked Ladies, The Weathercock, Masquerades], translated from the Danish by Henry Alexander, with an introduction by O. J. Campbell. Princeton University Press and The American-Scandinavian Foundation. Princeton, New Jersey. 1946.
Seven One-Act Plays by Holberg [The Talkative Barber, The Arabian Powder, The Christmas Party, Diderich the Terrible, The Peasant in Pawn, Sganarel's Journey to the Land of the Philosopher, The Changed Bridegroom], translated from the Danish by Henry

Alexander, with an introduction by Svend Kragh-Jacobsen. Princeton University Press and The American-Scandinavian Foundation. Princeton, New Jersey. 1950.

Three Comedies [The Transformed Peasant, The Arabian Powder, The Healing Spring], translation and introduction by Reginald Spink. Heinemann. London. 1957.

4. Niels Klim

Holberg's Latin travel romance has been translated three times into English:

Journey to the World Under-Ground, London. 1742. New editions 1746, 1749, 1772, 1812. This original translation has been used as the basis of the most recent edition:

The Journey of Niels Klim to the World Underground. Introduced and edited by James I. McNab, Jr. University of Nebraska. Lincoln. 1960.

Journey to the World Under Ground. London. 1828.

Niels Klim's Journey under the Ground, translated by John Gierlow. Boston and New York. 1845.

5. Historical Writings

Holberg's major historical works have never been available to an English-speaking readership. However, his two elementary textbooks in Latin, *Synopsis Historiæ Universalis,* 1733, and *Compendium Geographicum,* 1733, have been translated and somewhat expanded in English:

An Introduction to Universal History. Translated from the Latin of Baron Holberg. With notes, historical, chronological and critical. By Gregory Sharpe. London. 1755. 2nd edition, corrected and enlarged. To which is added A Short System of Geography, with maps etc. London. 1758. New edition, revised, corrected and improved by William Radcliffe. London. 1787.

6. Epistles

Selected Essays of Ludvig Holberg. Translated from the *Epistler* with an introduction and notes by P. M. Mitchell. University of Kansas Press. Lawrence. 1955.

7. Moral Thoughts

This important work has never been translated into English. Now, however, one chapter of it has appeared in:

Anthology of Danish Literature. Bilingual Edition. Edited by F. J.
Billeskov Jansen and P. M. Mitchell. Southern Illinois University
Press, Carbondale and Edwardsville. Feffer and Simons, London
and Amsterdam. 1971.

SECONDARY SOURCES

Literature in English about Holberg

BILLESKOV JANSEN, F. J.: "Ludvig Holberg and Some French Think-
ers." In *Scandinavian Studies; Essays Presented to Dr. Henry
Goddard Leach.* Seattle. 1965.
CAMPBELL, OSCAR JAMES: *The Comedies of Holberg.* Harvard Uni-
versity Press. Cambridge. 1914.
MITCHELL, P. M.: *A History of Danish Literature.* Copenhagen 1957.
New York 1958. Second, augmented edition. New York. 1971.

Some Danish and Norwegian Works on Holberg

BILLESKOV JANSEN, F. J.: *Holberg som Epigrammatiker og Essayist*
I–II. Copenhagen. 1938–39.
BULL, FRANCIS: *Holberg som historiker.* Oslo. 1913.
FOSS, KÅRE: *Konge for en dag.* Et socialpolitisk teatermotiv. Oslo. 1960.
KRUUSE, JENS: *Holbergs maske.* Copenhagen. 1964.
MÜLLER, TH. A.: *Den unge Ludvig Holberg 1684–1722.* Copen-
hagen. 1943.
SPANG-HANSSEN, EBBE: *Erasmus Montanus og naturvidenskaben.*
Copenhagen. 1965.
THOMSEN, EJNAR: *Sfinxen-Streger til et Holberg-portræt.* Copen-
hagen 1954.

Index

Adeler, Cort, 22
Alexander the Great, 64
Andersen, Hans Christian, 13, 19, 74, 110
Aristophanes, 61
Arnold, Gottfried, 116

Bartholin, Hans, 36
Bayle, Pierre, 17, 39, 111, 112, 118
Berg, Christian, 109
Bidermann, Jacob, 63
Bignon, Jean-Paul de, 38
Boileau, 47, 49, 54, 55
Boissy, Louis de, 109
Boleyn, Anne, 97
Bormann, Johannes, 38
Bossuet, 37, 96
Boursault, 73
Brahe, Tycho, 46
Brix, Christian, 26, 27
Brorson, Hans Adolph, 18, 20, 21, 126

Caesar, 97
Capion, Etienne, 60
Castel, Louis-Bertrand, 38, 80
Chamberlayne, Edward, 89, 90
Christian, Prince of Denmark, 58
Christian II, King of Denmark, 92
Christian III, King of Denmark, 31
Christian IV, King of Denmark, 13, 25, 30, 31, 32, 56, 57, 58, 93
Christian V, King of Denmark, 14, 30, 31
Christian VI, King of Denmark, 15, 61, 98, 106, 108
Christian X, King of Denmark, 21
Chrysostom, John, 86
Clement XI, 40

Cleopatra, 97
Cicero, 39, 97, 102, 103, 104
Confucius, 107
Copernicus, 46
Corneille, 55
Coyet, Gustav Wilhelm, 61, 62
Crates, 118
Cromwell, 58

Dalin, Olof, 117
Democritus, 53
Demosthenes, 39, 97
Descartes, 17
Destouches, 109

Eckenberg, J. C., 60
Eigtved, Nicolai, 16, 109
Elizabeth I, Queen of England, 97
Eugene, Prince of Savoy, 30

Fabricius, Johann Albert, 84
Faustus, Dr., 115
Fleury, Cardinal, 113
Francke, A. H., 98
Frederik II, King of Denmark, 56, 57, 124
Frederik III, King of Denmark, 14, 25, 30, 31, 32, 92, 94, 98
Frederik IV, King of Denmark, 14, 15, 31, 45, 59, 61, 95, 98
Frederik V, King of Denmark, 15, 16, 108

Goldsmith, Oliver, 85
Gram, Hans, 36, 84
Gregory VII, 113
Griffenfeld, 93
Grotius, Hugo, 33
Grubbe, Marie, 118

133

Grundtvig, N. F. S., 96
Gustavus II Adolphus, King of Sweden, 13

Hagen, Aage, 123
Harder, Henrik, 107
Hardouin, 80
Hegelund, Peder Jensen, 57
Heraclitus, 53
Herodian, 108, 111
Hipparchia, 118
Hobbes, Thomas, 34
Hojer, Andreas, 31, 44, 45, 49
Holberg, Christian Nielsen, 22, 72
Holberg, Sophie, 23
Holstein, U. A., 60
Homer, 48, 49, 77
Horace, 54, 88, 105
Hostrup, Jens Christian, 68

Jacobsen, J. P., 118
Juvenal, 46, 47

Keigwin, R. P., 20
Kierkegaard, Søren, 19, 74
Krogh, Thomas Georg, 85

Lauremberg, Johannes, 58
Leibniz, 72, 99, 112, 127
Lem, Karen, 22
Lem, Niels Pedersen, 22
Lem, Peder, 22, 23
Lintrup, Søren, 23
Locke, John, 99
Londemann, Gert, 108
Louis XIV, 14, 30, 37, 39, 89, 90
Louis-Joseph, duc de Vendôme, 30
Louise, Queen of Denmark, 108
Luther, 96
Lyschander, Claus Christoffersen, 31

Magnússon, Árni, 22
Marcus Aurelius, 108
Margaret I, Queen of Denmark, 92, 97
Marivaux, 80
Martial, 107
Melancthon, Philip, 33

Mencke, Johann Burkhard, 45
Molesworth, Robert, 91
Molière, 55, 57, 59, 60, 61, 62, 73, 79, 85, 109
Montaigne, 74, 102, 103, 104
Montaigu, Rene Magnon de, 59, 60
Montesquieu, 14, 99, 119, 120, 121, 122
Munthe, Ludvig, 23
Müller, Johann Georg, 85

Nemeitz, J. C., 38
Newton, Isaac, 17

Orsini, Cardinal, 117
Ovid, 80, 103
Owen, John, 107

Paulli, Joachim Richard, 74, 75
Peter the Great, 100, 120
Pflug, H. O., 29
Plautus, 61, 68, 72, 110
Pliny the Younger, 83, 95
Plutarch, 96
Pontoppidan, Erik, 106
Pufendorf, Samuel, 29, 30, 32, 33, 34, 45

Qvoten, Julius von, 109
Qvoten, Salomon von, 60, 77

Racine, 55, 78
Ranch, Hieronymus Justesen, 57
Rapin, Paul de Thoyras, 92
Rathler, E. L., 84
Regnard, 109
Reitzer, Christian, 30, 32, 33
Resen, Peder Hansen, 31
Reuss, Heinrich, 124
Riccoboni, Luigi, 79
Rosenkrantz, Iver, 36
Rostgaard, Frederik, 26, 31, 60
Rousseau, 14, 85
Rudbeck, Olof, 117
Rømer, Ole, 46

Sallust, 103
Samson, 57

Saxo, 45, 93
Schnabel, Bernard, 38
Schrader, Johann Herman, 18
Sehested, Hannibald, 93
Seneca, 102, 104, 105
Sevel, J. J., 26
Shakespeare, 57
Simon, Richard, 111
Skeel, Mogens, 59
Smed, Niels, 24
Socrates, 97
Solomon, 57
Spener, P. J., 98
Stoud, Ludvig, 23
Stoud, Otto, 25, 26
Stoud, Sophie, 26
Stromsoe, Bergliot, 49
Stub, Ambrosius, 16
Suhm, Peter Frederik, 111
Sulla, 78, 97
Swift, 99
Syv, Peder, 104, 105

Terence, 61
Thielo, C. A., 108, 109
Thomasius, Christian, 33, 99
Trolle, Herluf, 124

Ulfeldt, Corfitz, 93
Ursin, Georg, 27

Vedel, Anders Sørensen, 93
Virgil, 47, 48, 49, 103
Voltaire, 14, 90, 123, 126, 127

Wallenstein, 13, 58
Wegner, Henrik, 78
Weile, Christen Osterson, 22
Weinwich, Christen, 24
Winding, Poul, 29
Winsløw, Jakob, 37
Wolff, Christian, 70
Wright, Edward, 40
Wøldike, Marcus, 95

Zeno, 117

DATE DUE

GAYLORD			PRINTED IN U.S.A.